Horizons

Phonics and Reading

K

Teacher's Guide 1
Lessons 1–40

Author: Pollyann O'Brien, M.A.

Editor: Alan L. Christopherson, M.S.

Alpha Omega Publications, Inc. • Rock Rapids, IA

Printed in the United States of America

ISBN 978-0-7403-0146-9

Table of Contents

Introduction

Introduction

The *Horizons Kindergarten Phonics and Reading* program for Grade K is designed to help lay the foundation that students will need for reading success. It is an organized program in which letter-sound correspondences are directly taught and blended. These sounds are practiced in words, word lists, word families, and in short sentences. In this program students are taught concepts, not words. The focus for this material is on the phonics and on the reading. Penmanship and spelling are also practiced but will be covered in more detail in the materials for Grade 1. The program has three major components: the **Student Workbooks**, the **Teacher's Guides**, and the **Readers**.

The Student Workbooks

Horizons Phonics and Reading K, Book 1, contains Lessons 1–40.
Horizons Phonics and Reading K, Book 2, contains Lessons 41–80.
Horizons Phonics and Reading K, Book 3, contains Lessons 81–120.
Horizons Phonics and Reading K, Book 4, contains Lessons 121–160.

The Teacher's Guides

Horizons Phonics and Reading K, Teacher's Guide 1, Lessons 1–40.
Horizons Phonics and Reading K, Teacher's Guide 2, Lessons 41–80.
Horizons Phonics and Reading K, Teacher's Guide 3, Lessons 81–120.
Horizons Phonics and Reading K, Teacher's Guide 4, Lessons 121–160.

The Readers

Ann's Cat, Horizons Phonics and Reading K Reader 1, contains stories for Lessons 1–40.
Mike's Bike, Horizons Phonics and Reading K Reader 2, contains stories for Lessons 41–80.
Clem's Snake, Horizons Phonics and Reading K Reader 3, contains stories for Lessons 81–120.
Van's Scarecrow, Horizons Phonics and Reading K Reader 4, contains stories for Lessons 121–159.

Lesson Preparation

The *Horizons Phonics and Reading K Program* contains a total of 160 lessons. Typically, one lesson should be completed each day during the school year. Prepare for each day by carefully reviewing the material provided in the *Teacher's Guide*. The **Overview** is a summary of the concepts that will be covered in the lesson. Also review the **Scope and Sequence**, found in the front of each *Teacher's Guide* to see what concepts will be taught in future lessons. The **Materials and Supplies** is a list what will be needed for the lesson. Get these items assembled before starting class with the students. Since many will be used for several lessons you may choose to hang them on the wall or on a bulletin board. The **Teaching Tips** are classroom-teaching procedures that give special instructions for each activity of the lesson. Take your time in going over these procedures. Thoroughly think through what you will say and do, so that you have a plan in your mind before teaching the lesson to the students. The **Answer Keys** are reduced student pages with answers. These pages allow you to have both the **Teacher Notes** and the **Student pages** in front of as you teach the lesson.

It will be necessary to go over most of the pictures in the workbook with the students. Tell them what word each of the pictures illustrates. The students are to complete the activity after you have gone over the pictures and the words. Allow sufficient time for the students to do the activity before going on to the next. Compliment and encourage the students as they work.

Each Lesson has at least 4 pages of student activities. Doing all four of these pages at one sitting is not necessary or recommended. Do the first two pages and then take a break or work in another subject. After the break, pass out the second set of pages. Do some review and then complete the lesson with the students. Each group of students is different, so be flexible and vary the routine.

The Readers

The stories in the readers are to be covered after the student lesson has been completed. The story will illustrate and demonstrate the primary concept of the lesson. Most kindergarten students should not be expected to read these stories independently the first time they are used. The stories include a mixture of simple short-vowel words and more complex multi-syllable or long-vowel words. Read the stories to the students, pausing where appropriate to allow the students to sound out and read the words they have covered in the lessons. As the students become more proficient at sounding out words, you can drop back and repeat earlier stories that the students should be able to read more independently.

Floor Puzzle

Included with this program is a large floor puzzle of the 26 letters of the alphabet. It is suggested that you glue this to heavier stock and/or laminate it before cutting the letters out. The individual letters can be used as flashcards or put together as a puzzle.

Student Wipe-off Tablet

Included with this program is a lined wipe-off tablet for the students to use. As you demonstrate letters and words on the white board, the students can practice the same on their tablets.

Alphabet flow chart

This manipulative is to be made or purchased by the teacher or parent. It is simply a set of alphabet flashcards that can be displayed and hung on the top of the white board one letter at a time, as the letters are learned in the workbooks. As an alternative you can use the **Floor Puzzle** pieces and clip them to a clothesline or hang them on hooks. Whatever is done, keep at least one set of letters available to use for flashcards.

Alphabet Story and Alphabet Poem

In the back of this guide there is an Alphabet Story, an Alphabet Poem, and a set of illustrations. The illustrations correlate to both the poem and story. Copies of the illustrations can be made so they can be used as flashcards while reciting the poem or story. The phrases of the poem and the sentences of the story contain words that highlight the letters of the alphabet. Use the poem and story as a daily review of the letters that have been covered and as a way to practice the sounds made by the letters.

Curriculum Overview

Horizons Kindergarten Phonics is a phonetically based word-recognition and early reading program. There is a strong emphasis placed on comprehension and language arts skills. Students learn to identify the name and sounds of each letter through picture association with a sequential alphabet story.

The use of each individual letter sound blended into words is further reinforced by pictures and printing the letter names. Sentences and stories are introduced immediately. Dolch sight words are incorporated so that comprehension is enhanced. In addition to the reading section, much emphasis is placed on the following:

- spelling
- alphabetizing
- rhyming
- vocabulary development
- sentence structure including statement, question, and exclamation sentences
- puzzle and make-up words, phrases and sentences for accurate decoding
- auditory skills in recognizing a spoken word
- sequence
- diacritical markings
- complete sentence identification
- nouns
- verbs
- pronouns
- apostrophe for possession
- contractions
- realistic choices: yes or no – could be or could not be

There are several activities associated with each skill. The teacher can choose to expand on the skill by utilizing the accumulation of words for each segment. By using the puzzle approach on the white board with easy-erase markers, a teacher can review and expand the material within the lesson. Underneath each skill name in the **Scope and Sequence** is the list of activities that are included with that skill.

Reading: The First Chapter In Education

No other skill taught in school and learned by school children is more important than reading. It is the gateway to all other knowledge. If children do not learn to read efficiently, the path is blocked to every subject they encounter in their school years.

The past five years have brought major breakthroughs in our knowledge of how children learn to read and why so many fail. These new insights have been translated into techniques for teaching reading to beginning readers, including the many students who would otherwise encounter difficulties in mastering this fundamental skill. Researchers have come to appreciate that early identification and treatment of such students can make all the difference. Researchers have also documented the problems — personal, social, and educational — that too often result when early attention and intervention do not occur.

Reading to Learn

Students who do not "learn to read" during the first three years of school experience enormous difficulty when they are subsequently asked to "read to learn." Teaching students to read by the end of third grade is the single most important task assigned to elementary schools. During the first three years of schooling, students "learn to read." That is, they develop the capacity to interpret the written symbols for the oral language that they have been hearing since birth. Starting in fourth grade, schooling takes on a very different purpose, one that in many ways is more complex and demanding of higher-order thinking skills. If efficient reading skills are not developed by this time, the English language, history, mathematics, current events, and the rich tapestries of literature and science become inaccessible.

In addition, a strong body of evidence shows that most students who fall behind in reading skills never catch up with their peers and become fluent readers. They fall further and further behind in school, become frustrated, and drop out at much higher rates than their classmates. They find it difficult to obtain rewarding employment and are effectively prevented from drawing on the power of education to improve and enrich their lives. Researchers speak of this syndrome as the "Matthew Effect" — the rich get richer and the poor get poorer.

Most Americans know how central reading is to education. According to a 1994 poll conducted by Peter D. Hart Research Associates, nearly 70 percent of teachers believe that reading is the "most important" skill for children to learn. Two years earlier, the same polling firm reported that 62 percent of parents believed that reading was one of the most important skills for their children to master. Both teachers and parents ranked reading as more critical than mathematics and computer skills. In other words, there is general agreement among researchers and the public that all children must learn to read early in their academic careers.

The Challenges of Illiteracy

More students fail to learn to read by the end of the third grade than many people imagine. Indeed, it is no exaggeration to say that all schools encounter students who fall into this category and that all schools should have plans for addressing the special needs of these students.

In its 1994 Reading Assessment, the National Assessment of Education Progress (NAEP), a federally supported program that tracks the performance of American students in core academic subjects, reported that more than four out of 10 fourth-graders (42 percent) in American schools were reading at a "below basic" level. This means that they could not understand "uncomplicated narratives and high-interest informative texts." NAEP also reported that such illiteracy persists in the higher grades. The report found that nearly one-third (31 percent) of eighth-graders and nearly one-third (30 percent) of twelfth-graders are also reading at a "below basic" level. The latter figures probably understate the problem, because many poor readers drop out of school before twelfth grade.

Other researchers have come to similar conclusions regarding how widespread students' reading problems really are. National longitudinal studies have measured the ability of children to recognize individual words in text. Their data suggest that more than one child in six (17.5 percent) will encounter a problem in learning to read during the crucial first three years of school. Further evidence comes from the sharp rise in the number of students who are diagnosed as learning disabled or are referred to special education because they cannot read at the proper grade level.

In contrast to popular belief, reading failure is not concentrated among particular types of schools or among specific groups of students. To the contrary, students who have difficulty reading represent a virtual cross-section of American children. They include rich and poor, male and female, rural and urban, and public and private school children in all sections of the country. According to the NAEP assessment, for example, nearly one-third (32 percent) of fourth graders whose parents graduated from college are reading at the "below basic" level.

In short, the failure of a substantial number of students to learn to read during the critical first three years of school is a national problem—one that confronts every community and every school in the country.

A Common Stumbling Block: Phonemic Awareness

Whatever the reason children fail to read by the end of the third grade, most non-readers share a common problem. They have not developed the capacity to recognize what reading experts call phonemes. Phonemes are the smallest units of speech—the basic building blocks of speaking and writing. The word "cat," for example, contains three phonemes: the /k/, /a/, and /t/ sounds. Phonemes are often identical to individual letters, but not always. The word "ox," for example, has two letters but three phonemes: the /o/, /k/, and /s/ sounds.

Researchers have demonstrated that accomplished readers are adept at recognizing phonemes and putting them together to construct words and phrases. They do this quickly, accurately, and automatically. The absence of this critical linguistic skill makes it difficult for children to decode and read single words, much less sentences, paragraphs, and whole stories. Teaching phonemic awareness and discrimination among phonemes is imperative for all students.

Solutions in the Classroom

Teaching beginners to read must be highly purposeful and strategic. Effective techniques have been developed for helping students, including those with learning disabilities, to develop phonological awareness, word recognition, and other advanced skills required for reading.

Phonological awareness activities build on and enhance children's experiences with written (e.g., print awareness) and spoken language (e.g., playing with words). A beginning reader with successful phonological awareness and knowledge of letters ostensibly learns how words are represented in print.

Intervention for learners who have difficulty with phonological awareness must be early, strategic, systematic, and carefully designed. It must be based on a curriculum that recognizes and balances the importance of both phonics instruction and the appreciation of meaning.

For children who have difficulty reading, effective reading instruction strategies should be used to build phonological awareness and alphabetic understanding. These strategies should be explicit, making phonemes prominent in children's attention and perception. For example, teachers can model specific sounds and in turn ask the children to produce the sounds. In addition, opportunities to engage in phonological awareness activities should be plentiful, frequent, and fun.

Instructional strategies should consider the characteristics that make a word easier or more difficult to read. These include: the number of phonemes in the word; phoneme position in words (initial sounds are easier); phonological properties of words (e.g., continuants, such as /m/, are easier than stop sounds, such as /t/); and phonological awareness dimensions, including blending sounds, segmenting words, and rhyming.

Many early readers will require greater teacher assistance and support. Using a research-based strategy known as scaffolding, teachers should provide students with lots of instructional support in the beginning stages of reading instruction, and gradually reduce the support as students learn more about reading skills. The ultimate goal is for students to read on their own without the help of a teacher.

A Balanced Approach

Unfortunately, it is not always easy for teachers to recognize students with reading difficulties. When they do, teachers sometimes find themselves caught between conflicting schools of thought about how to treat reading disabilities. One school of thought gives considerable attention to the teaching of phonics in the early stages of reading. Another school of thought emphasizes the whole language approach. Should teachers rely on phonics instruction, whole language instruction, or a combination of the two?

The U.S. Department of Education and the National Institute of Child Health and Human Development (NICHD) have supported the review of hundreds of studies done in recent years on reading instruction and disabilities. This body of research suggests that the relatively recent swing away from phonics instruction to a singular whole language approach is making it more difficult to lift children with learning disabilities out of the downward learning spiral and, in fact, may impede the progress of many students in learning to read with ease.

Few dispute the value of giving children opportunities to write, surrounding children with good literature, and generally creating a rich literate environment for students. But for many children this is not enough. Such children will have continued difficulty with reading unless they master the decoding skills associated with phonics instruction.

Research makes clear that children do not learn to read the way they learn to talk. Speech is a natural human capacity, and learning to talk requires little more than exposure and opportunity. In contrast, written language is an artifact, a human invention, and reading is not a skill that can be acquired through immersion alone. Beginning readers benefit from instruction that helps them understand that the words they speak and hear can be represented by written symbols — and that letters and the sounds associated with them, when combined and recombined, form words — just as they benefit from experiences that make reading fun.

California's experience with a chosen reading approach is instructive. A decade ago, the state became a leader in the movement to embrace whole language instruction. However, as a result of low reading scores, a task force was formed and has recently adopted a more balanced reading approach that includes building phonological awareness along with the reading of meaningful and engaging texts.

Research indicates that reading can be taught effectively with a balanced approach that uses the best of both teaching approaches. Such an approach incorporates phonics instruction with the rich literacy environments advocated by whole language instruction.

Reading: The Key to Success

As already discussed, reading is the gateway to learning. Facility to understand and use written language has always been a prerequisite to the efficient acquisition of knowledge, and it is becoming increasingly important in today's information society. In the past, it may have been possible for persons who were illiterate to obtain a good job, support a family, and live a comfortable life, but those days are gone. Children who do not learn to read today can expect to live on the margins of society in every way.

Scope & Sequence

Lesson 1

Letter **a**

- letter recognition
- short **a** sound
- recognizing and forming uppercase and lowercase **a**

Lesson 2

Letter **b**

- letter recognition
- beginning and ending letter **b** sound
- sound of **ba**
- recognizing and forming uppercase and lowercase **b**

Lesson 3

Letter **d**

- letter recognition
- letter **d** sound
- sound of **dă**
- recognizing and forming uppercase and lowercase **d**

Lesson 4

Letter **o**

- letter recognition
- beginning sound of short **o**
- recognizing and forming uppercase and lowercase **o**
- sound of **lŏ**
- words with short **o** in the middle
- formation of **ba**, **bo**, **do**, **dad**

Lesson 5

Letter **c**

- letter recognition
- sound of letter **c**
- words beginning with **c** and **că**
- recognizing and forming uppercase and lowercase **c**
- formation of **co**, **ca**

Lesson 6

Letter **e**

- letter recognition
- sound of short **e**
- words with **ĕ** in the middle
- matching phrases to pictures
- beginning sounds **dĕ** and **bĕ**
- word recognition and matching
- recognizing and forming uppercase and lowercase **e**
- matching letter to pictures starting with **ĕ**

Lesson 7

Letter **f**

- letter recognition
- sound of **f**
- beginning sounds **f**, **fă**, **fĕ**
- recognizing and forming uppercase and lowercase **f**
- reading and writing "make-up words"
- reading and writing short sentences

Lesson 8

Letter **g**

- letter recognition
- beginning sounds **g**, **gă**, **gŏ**
- words beginning and ending in **g**
- auditory discrimination from word list
- recognizing and forming uppercase and lowercase **g**
- matching letter to pictures starting with **g**
- reading and writing "make-up words"
- reading and writing short sentences

Lesson 9

Letter **i**

- letter recognition
- beginning sound of short **i**
- words with short **i** in the middle
- beginning consonant sounds
- middle vowel sounds
- recognizing and forming uppercase and lowercase **i**
- matching letter to pictures starting with **i**

Lesson 10

Letter **h**

- letter recognition
- beginning sounds **h, hă, hě, hŏ, hĭ**
- recognizing and forming uppercase and lowercase **h**
- reading and writing "make-up words"
- matching letter to pictures starting with **h**
- adding **s** to make plurals
- capital letter at beginning and period at end of sentence
- matching pictures to phrases

Lesson 11

Letter **u**

- letter recognition
- beginning sounds of **ŭ, dŭ, fŭ, bŭ, cŭ, gŭ**
- words with **ŭ** in the middle
- recognizing and forming uppercase and lowercase **u**
- matching letter to pictures with **ŭ** in the middle
- matching pictures to words

Lesson 12

Letter **t**

- letter recognition
- beginning and ending sound of **t**
- recognizing and forming uppercase and lowercase **t**
- matching letter to pictures starting with **t**
- reading and writing "make-up words"
- reading and printing sentences
- matching pictures to phrases
- recognition and printing **ta, te, ti, to, tu**

Lesson 13

Letter **n**

- letter recognition
- sound of **n, nă**
- matching pictures to words
- recognizing and forming uppercase and lowercase **n**

- matching letters to words starting with **n**
- spelling words to match pictures
- completing sentences with correct word
- printing words and phrases from copy
- identifying pictures starting with **ne, ni, nu, no**
- identifying pictures starting with **an, en, in, un**

Lesson 14

Letter **k**

- letter recognition
- beginning sounds **k, kĭ, kě**
- matching pictures to phrases
- recognizing and forming uppercase and lowercase **k**
- printing letters and words with **k**
- reading "make-up words"
- reading and printing sentences

Lesson 15

Letter **l**

- letter recognition
- beginning sounds **l, lă, lě, lĭ, lŏ, lŭ**
- ending sound of **l**
- recognizing and forming uppercase and lowercase **l**
- printing letters and words
- completing sentences with correct word
- reading "make-up words"

Lesson 16

Letter **m**

- recognizing and forming uppercase and lowercase **m**
- completing sentences with correct word
- spelling words to match pictures
- reading "make-up words"
- matching pictures to beginning sounds **ma, me, mi, mo, mu**
- reading and printing words and phrases from copy

Horizons Kindergarten Phonics and Reading

Lesson 17

Letter **p**

- recognizing and forming uppercase and lowercase **p**
- beginning sounds of **pa**, **pe**, **pi**, **po**, **pu**
- matching pictures to words
- matching letters to words starting with **p**
- reading "make-up words"
- spelling words to match pictures
- printing words and phrases from copy
- completing sentences with correct word

Lesson 18

Letter **r**

- recognizing and forming uppercase and lowercase **r**
- matching letters to words starting with **r**
- reading "make-up words"
- beginning sounds of **ra**, **re**, **ri**, **ro**, **ru**
- matching pictures to words
- completing sentences with correct word
- spelling words to match pictures
- printing words and phrases from copy

Lesson 19

Letter **s**

- recognizing and forming uppercase and lowercase **s**
- matching letters to words starting with **s**
- beginning sounds of **sa**, **se**, **si**, **so**, **su**
- matching pictures to phrases
- recognizing ending sound of **s**
- printing letters, words, and phrases
- completing sentences with correct word

Lesson 20

Letter **q**

- recognizing and forming uppercase and lowercase **q**, **qu**, **qui**
- matching letters to words starting with **qu**
- match pictures to words
- reading and writing sentences

Lesson 21

Letter **j**

- recognizing and forming uppercase and lowercase **j**
- matching letters to words starting with **j**
- matching pictures to words
- completing sentences with correct word
- matching pictures to phrases
- beginning sounds of **ja**, **je**, **ji**, **jo**, **ju**
- spelling words to match pictures
- printing words and phrases from copy

Lesson 22

Letter **v**

- recognizing and forming uppercase and lowercase **v**
- matching letters to words starting with **v**
- spelling words to match pictures
- matching pictures to words and phrases
- beginning sounds of **va**, **ve**, **vi**, **vo**, **vu**
- completing sentences with correct word
- printing words and phrases from copy
- spelling words to match pictures

Lesson 23

Letter **w**

- recognizing and forming uppercase and lowercase **w**
- matching letters to words starting with **w**
- reading "make-up words"
- matching pictures to words and phrases
- printing words from copy
- completing sentences with correct word
- spelling words to match pictures
- reading and printing sentences

Lesson 24

Letter **y**

- recognizing and forming uppercase and lowercase **y**
- printing letters and words
- matching letters to words starting with **y**
- matching pictures to words and phrases

- completing sentences with correct word
- spelling words to match pictures

Lesson 25

Letter **z**

- recognizing and forming uppercase and lowercase **z**
- matching letters to words starting with **z**
- matching pictures to words
- reading "make-up words"
- recognizing words that end in **z**
- printing letters and words
- completing sentences with correct word
- printing phrases from copy

Lesson 26

Letter **x**

- recognizing and forming uppercase and lowercase **x**
- matching letters to words starting with **x**
- reading "make-up words"
- matching pictures to phrases, sentences, words
- words ending in **x**
- completing sentences with correct word
- spelling words to match pictures
- printing phrases from copy

Lesson 27

Consonant digraph **th**

- rule for beginning consonant digraph **th**
- matching picture to starting sound of **th**
- printing uppercase/lowercase **th**
- reading words/sentences
- identifying puzzle words and phrases
- rhyming and spelling
- reading and printing sentences from copy

Lesson 28

Consonant digraph **th**

- recognize **th** at the beginning or end of a word
- matching pictures to sentences

- printing sentences from copy
- reading "make-up" words
- puzzle words/phrases
- rhyming
- crossword puzzle with missing vowel

Lesson 29

Consonant digraph **ch**

- rule for consonant digraph **ch**
- matching pictures to sound
- using capital letters for names
- printing uppercase/lowercase **ch**
- proper nouns
- reading sentences
- matching words/pictures
- matching puzzle words and phrases
- spelling

Lesson 30

Consonant digraph **wh**

- rule for consonant digraph **wh**
- identify capital and lowercase letters
- identify nonsense words
- create nonsense words from sounds
- printing sentences from copy
- spelling
- use of question mark (?) and words to identify question sentences

Lesson 31

Review **th, ch, wh**

- picture/word review
- picture to sound
- printing
- auditory discrimination from word list
- spelling
- puzzle/"make-up" words and sentences
- recognizing words starting with ch within sentences

Horizons Kindergarten Phonics and Reading

Lesson 32

Consonant digraph **sh**

- rule for beginning consonant digraph **sh**
- printing practice with capital and lowercase **sh**
- picture/word match
- puzzle/make-believe words and phrases
- word search
- printing sentences from copy
- rhyming
- spelling

Lesson 33

Consonant digraph **sh**

- rule for **sh** endings
- printing practice with and lowercase **sh**
- picture/beginning sound
- sentences to match picture
- rhyming
- alphabetize
- print sentences from copy
- identify sh at end of word

Lesson 34

Review consonant digraphs **th, ch, wh, sh**

- picture/sound identification
- printing/identifying ending sound
- word/picture identification
- auditory discrimination from word list
- spelling
- printing from copy

Lesson 35

Silent **e**: ā ȼ

- rule for silent **e: a ȼ**
- picture to sound
- diacritical marking
- short/long **a** contrast
- picture/sentence match
- puzzle/make-believe words and phrases
- spelling
- sentence completion
- word identification without pictures

Lesson 36

Consonant blend **bl**

- rule for blend **bl**
- picture to sound
- printing practice with capital and lowercase **bl**
- printing from copy
- picture to sentence match
- spelling
- word to picture match
- puzzle/make-believe words and phrases
- beginning blend choice

Lesson 37

Consonant blend **br**

- rule for blend **br**
- picture to sound
- printing practice with capital and lowercase **br**
- word identification – diacritical marking
- word/picture identification of sound
- sentence to picture match
- puzzle/make-believe words and sentences
- spelling
- sentence completion
- printing sentence from copy

Lesson 38

Consonant blend **cl**

- rule for blend **cl**
- picture to sound
- printing practice with capital and lowercase **cl**
- word/picture identification for printing
- beginning blend printing/spelling
- picture to word match
- puzzle/make-believe words and phrases
- printing sentence from copy

Lesson 39

Consonant blend **cr**

- rule for consonant blend **cr**
- picture to sound
- printing practice with capital and lowercase **cr**
- picture to word match
- printing beginning sounds
- word/picture identification for printing
- alphabetize
- sentence completion
- puzzle/make-believe words and phrases
- spelling

Lesson 40

Review consonant blends **cr**, **cl**, **br**, **bl**

- word/picture identification
- auditory discrimination from word list
- puzzle/make-believe words and phrases
- spelling – fill in beginning and ending sounds
- sentence printing from copy

Lesson 41

Silent **e**: $\bar{\text{i}}$ ¢

- rule for silent **e**: $\bar{\text{i}}$ ¢
- word/picture identification
- diacritical marking
- word/picture match
- sentence/picture match
- puzzle/make-believe words and phrases
- spelling

Lesson 42

Consonant blend **dr** – question sentences

- rule for consonant blend **dr**
- word/picture identification
- practice printing with capital and lowercase **dr**
- word/picture match
- printing beginning sounds for picture
- choice of beginning sounds
- puzzle/make-believe words and phrases

- rule for question marks and sentences
- review of question words and use of question marks
- spelling
- rhyming

Lesson 43

Consonant blend **fl**

- rule for consonant blend **fl**
- practice printing with capital and lowercase **fl**
- beginning sounds identified
- printing beginning sounds
- alphabetical order
- sentence completion
- puzzle/make-believe words and phrases
- sentence printing from copy

Lesson 44

Review silent **e**: $\bar{\text{a}}$ ¢ and $\bar{\text{i}}$ ¢ with single consonant beginnings

- review silent e rule
- diacritical marking
- picture/word identification
- printing – place in columns
- word/picture match
- auditory discrimination from word list
- spelling
- sentence completion

Lesson 45

Review silent **e**: $\bar{\text{a}}$ ¢ and $\bar{\text{i}}$ ¢ with consonant blend beginnings

- review silent **e** rule
- picture to sound – diacritical markings
- printing – place in columns
- word/picture match
- auditory discrimination from word list
- spelling
- sentence completion from pictures
- sentence completion – original

Lesson 46

Ending **ck**
- rule for **ck** ending
- picture/sound identification
- placement of sound within word
- picture/sentence match
- rhyming
- alphabetical order
- puzzle/make-believe words and phrases
- spelling

Lesson 47

Ending **ing**
- rule for **ing** ending
- picture to sound
- word identification
- picture to word match
- picture/sentence identification and printing
- word completion
- sentence completion
- printing
- auditory discrimination from word list

Lesson 48

Review short and long vowels
- short vowel identification
- long vowel identification
- word/picture match
- puzzle/make-believe words and phrases
- auditory discrimination for word list
- word comprehension from sentence
- spelling

Lesson 49

Silent **e**: $\bar{o}$ $\cancel{e}$ – filling in sentences
- rule of silent **e**: $\bar{o}$ $\cancel{e}$
- word/picture identification
- printing short and long vowel words - diacritical marking
- word ending choice from pictures
- auditory discrimination from word list

- sentence completion
- rhyming
- puzzle and make believe words
- printing from copy

Lesson 50

Consonant blend **gr**
- rule for consonant blend **gr**
- word/picture match
- practice printing capital and lowercase **gr**
- beginning sound identification
- word/picture match
- printing (spelling) beginning sounds from picture
- alphabetical order
- sentence completion
- puzzle/make-believe words and phrases
- word search

Lesson 51

Consonant blend **gl**
- rule for consonant blend **gl**
- word/picture match
- practice printing capital and lowercase **gl**
- beginning sound identification
- alphabetical order
- ending sound identification
- auditory discrimination from word list
- sentence completion
- printing sentence from copy

Lesson 52

Consonant blend **sp** – beginning and ending
- rule for consonant blend **sp**
- word/picture match – beginning **sp**
- practice printing **sp** with capital
- word/picture match – ending **sp**
- sentence/picture match
- puzzle/make-believe words and phrases
- spelling and rhyming
- printing sentence from copy

Lesson 53

Consonant digraph ending **tch** and **ch**

- rule for consonant digraph **tch** and **ch**
- word/picture identification of sound
- word/picture match
- discrimination of **ch** and **tch**
- puzzle/make-believe words and phrases
- spelling
- auditory discrimination from word list
- crossword puzzle
- sentence printing from copy

Lesson 54

Review short vowels and silent **e**: ā ¢, ī ¢, ō ¢

- vowel identification
- diacritical marking
- change words from short to long vowel sounds
- words in columns – long **o, i, a**
- word/picture match
- word/sentence match
- rhyming

Lesson 55

Silent **e**: ū ¢

- review silent **e** rule
- word/picture identification
- print words to match pictures – copy
- sentence completion
- puzzle/make-believe words and phrases
- spelling
- separate columns for long vowel sounds
- auditory discrimination from word list

Lesson 56

Review short and long vowels with blends

- word/picture identification
- beginning or end sound identification
- sentence completion
- rhyming
- printing question sentence from copy

Lesson 57

Review short and long vowels with consonant single and blend beginning

- beginning sound identification/word/ picture
- sentence completion
- printing sentence from copy

Lesson 58

Consonant endings **nd**, **nt** – nouns

- rule for consonant endings **nd**, **nt**
- word/picture identification
- printing
- consonant ending discrimination
- auditory discrimination from word list
- rule for nouns – person, thing
- noun identification
- noun recognition of name from sentences
- noun recognition of place from sentences
- word/picture comprehension choice

Lesson 59

Consonant ending **ng** – noun review

- word/picture identification
- printing
- ending sound identification from pictures
- auditory discrimination from word list
- noun identification
- sentence/picture comprehension choice
- rhyming
- printing sentence from copy

Lesson 60

Consonant ending **nk** – writing question sentences

- rule for consonant ending **nk**
- word/picture identification
- printing
- ending discrimination
- auditory discrimination from word list
- sentence completion
- rhyming

- yes/no to question sentences
- printing choice of question sentence

Lesson 61

Review consonant blends **ng**, **nk**, **nd**, **nt**
- word endings identification
- auditory discrimination from word list
- noun identification
- printing
- spelling
- alphabetical order

Lesson 62

Consonant blends **sc** and **sk** beginnings
- rule for consonant blends **sc** and **sk**
- word/picture identification – **sc**
- printing
- word/picture identification – **sk**
- auditory discrimination from word list
- picture/sentence comprehension
- nouns – sentence identification
- sentence comprehension, completion and identification from picture

Lesson 63

Consonant blend **sk** endings
- rule for consonant blend **sk** ending
- work/picture identification
- printing
- word/picture match
- auditory discrimination from word list
- rhyming
- word/picture identification
- spelling
- sentence/picture comprehension
- alphabetical order

Lesson 64

Consonant blend **mp** endings – sentences
- rule for consonant blend **mp** endings
- picture/word identification
- printing
- word/picture discrimination
- auditory discrimination

- rhyming
- rule for description of sentence structure
- exclamation sentences
- question sentences
- statement sentences
- printing choice of sentences from copy

Lesson 65

Consonant ending **lp** – question sentences
- picture/word association
- printing
- picture/word discrimination
- printing choice from pictures – punctuation – question mark – period
- introduction to action words
- writing from copy with choice of action words
- spelling
- auditory discrimination from word list

Lesson 66

Consonant ending **lk** – vocabulary
- rule for consonant ending **lk**
- picture/word discrimination
- spelling choice for sentence completion and comprehension
- auditory discrimination from word list
- word/picture match
- spelling – ending sounds
- picture/sentence comprehension
- printing sentences from copy – punctuation

Lesson 67

Review endings **sk**, **mp**, **lp**, **lk** with short vowels
- picture/ending sound identification
- printing
- spelling
- auditory discrimination from word list
- sentence completion
- alphabetical order

Lesson 68

Review consonant blends

- word/picture identification
- beginning or ending sound discrimination
- spelling
- alphabetical order
- sentence completion
- rhyming
- writing sentence from copy

Lesson 69

Beginning consonant blend **pl** – pronouns

- rule for consonant blend **pl**
- word/picture identification
- practice printing **pl** with capital and lowercase letters
- picture/word beginning sound identification
- picture/word match
- alphabetical order
- Review noun rule
- rule – pronoun
- read sentences – change from noun to pronoun
- write sentence from copy – identify pronoun

Lesson 70

Review beginning consonant blends

- picture/beginning sound identification
- printing
- noun identification
- pronoun identification
- creative sentence making

Lesson 71

Double vowels – **ai**

- rule for double vowels – **ai**
- picture/sound identification
- word/picture match
- print rhyming words from copy
- puzzle/make-believe words and phrases
- sentence completion

- spelling
- printing sentence from copy

Lesson 72

Consonant blends with **ai**

- picture/sound identification
- printing
- puzzle/make-believe words and phrases
- picture/word and sound discrimination
- sentence/picture match
- sentence completion
- alphabetical order

Lesson 73

Consonant blend beginnings **pr**, **tr** – quotation marks

- rule for consonant blend beginnings **pr** and **tr**
- picture/word sound discrimination
- printing
- pictures/choice of beginning sounds
- word/picture match
- rule for quotation marks.
- read sentences
- print sentences using quotation marks

Lesson 74

Consonant blend beginning **sl**

- rule for consonant blend **sl**
- picture/word sound discrimination
- practice printing letters – capital and lowercase
- picture/beginning sound association
- picture/word match
- spelling
- puzzle/make-believe words and phrases
- create puzzle words

Lesson 75

Consonant blend beginning **sm**

- rule for consonant blend **sm**
- picture/word sound discrimination

- practice printing letters – capital and lowercase
- word/picture match
- sentence/picture match
- rhyming
- quotation marks
- spelling
- alphabetical order

Lesson 76

Consonant blend **sn**
- rule for consonant blend **sn**
- picture/word sound discrimination
- practice printing letters – capital and lowercase
- word/picture match
- sentence/picture match
- rhyming
- picture/sentence comprehension
- auditory discrimination from word list

Lesson 77

Review of consonant blends and digraphs
- pictures/sound discrimination
- auditory discrimination from word list
- auditory discrimination identifying ending sounds

Lesson 78

Double vowels – **ea**
- rule for double vowels **ea**
- picture/sound identification
- picture – printing and diacritical marking
- picture/word match
- puzzle/make-believe words and phrases
- rhyming
- sentence completion
- spelling
- printing sentence from copy

Lesson 79

Double vowels – **ee**
- rule for double vowels **ee**
- picture/sound identification

- picture – printing and diacritical marking
- picture/word match
- rhyming
- puzzle/make-believe words and phrases
- sentence/picture match
- spelling
- printing sentence from copy

Lesson 80

Beginning **qu** – picture sequence
- rule for **qu**
- picture/sound identification
- practice printing with capital and lowercase
- picture/word match
- rhyming
- sentence/picture match
- picture sequence

Lesson 81

Beginning blend **scr** – picture sequence
- picture/sound identification
- practice printing with capital and lowercase
- picture/word match
- printing sentence from copy – quotation marks
- spelling
- sentence sequence
- yes/no questions

Lesson 82

Review of double vowels – beginning blends
- picture/sound identification
- auditory discrimination from word list
- spelling
- picture/sentence comprehension
- sentence completion

Lesson 83

Double vowels – **oa**
- review double vowel rule – include **oa**
- picture/sound identification
- printing – diacritical marking

- word/picture match
- rhyming
- puzzle/make-believe words and phrases
- sentence comprehension/pictures
- spelling
- printing sentence from copy

Lesson 84

Beginning blend **fr**

- rule for beginning blend **fr**
- picture/sound identification
- practice printing with capital and lowercase
- picture/word match
- rhyming
- puzzle/make-believe words and phrases
- printing for sentence completion
- spelling
- yes/no sentence
- printing sentence from copy

Lesson 85

Consonant endings **lt, lf**

- rule for consonant ending **lt** and **lf**
- picture/sound identification
- reading – sentence comprehension
- auditory discrimination
- spelling
- printing – punctuation
- picture/sentence match

Lesson 86

Consonant ending **ft** – following directions

- rule for consonant ending **ft**
- picture/sound identification
- printing
- word ending sound identification
- auditory discrimination from word list
- picture/sentence comprehension
- follow directions
- word/picture match

Lesson 87

Review consonant endings

- pictures/sound identification
- sentence completion
- rhyme/picture
- auditory discrimination from word list
- spelling

Lesson 88

Review long and short vowel sounds

- picture/sound identification
- change word from short to long – diacritical marking
- column choice for words
- sentence completion

Lesson 89

Consonant blend beginnings **spr, spl**

- rule for consonant blend beginnings **spr, spl**
- picture/sound identification
- practice printing with capital and lowercase
- picture/sound discrimination
- word to word match
- read sentences from copy – print quotation marks
- alphabetical order
- sentence sequence for story

Lesson 90

Consonant blend beginning **st**

- rule for consonant blend beginning **st**
- picture/sound identification
- practice printing with capital and lowercase
- picture/word match
- rhyming
- puzzle/make-believe words and phrases
- sentence completion
- yes/no choice
- spelling

Lesson 91

Consonant blend review – **tch, sp, ft**
- ending sound identification
- printing
- picture/sentence comprehension match
- read sentences – vocabulary comprehension
- rhyming
- yes/no choice
- printing sentence from copy

Lesson 92

Consonant blend ending **st**
- rule for consonant blend ending **st**
- printing
- picture/sound identification
- auditory discrimination from word list
- rhyming
- reading sentences – vocabulary enrichment
- spelling
- sentence completion

Lesson 93

Review consonant endings – **tch, sp, st, lt, lf, ft**
- picture/sound identification
- auditory discrimination from word list
- sentence completion
- rhyming
- spelling – end sounds
- sentence choice to match picture

Lesson 94

Consonant blends **tw, sw**
- picture/sound identification
- puzzle/make-believe words and sentences
- printing sentence from copy
- sentence completion
- yes/no choice
- spelling

Lesson 95

Review consonant beginnings **tw, sp, st, spl, spr, qu**
- picture/sound identification
- auditory discrimination from word list
- sentence completion
- rhyming
- spelling
- yes/no choice
- alphabetical order
- print sentences – quotation marks

Lesson 96

Review endings **lf, ft, ng, nk, lk, lp, sk, sh**
- picture/sound discrimination
- sentence completion
- alphabetical order
- spelling
- could be/no way
- columns for endings
- read sentences – vocabulary development

Lesson 97

Vowel plus **r: ar**
- rule for vowel plus **r: ar**
- picture/sound identification
- practice printing with lowercase
- sentence/picture match – **ar** recognition
- rhyming
- puzzle/make-believe words and phrases
- read sentences – vocabulary development
- word search

Lesson 98

Vowel plus **r: or**
- rule for vowel plus **r: or**
- picture/sound identification
- practice printing with lowercase
- sentence/picture match – **or** recognition
- puzzle/make-believe words and phrases
- read sentences – vocabulary development
- sentence completion
- printing sentences – capitals/punctuation

Lesson 99

Review vowel plus **r**: **ar, or**

- picture/sound identification
- practice printing
- sentence completion
- alphabetical order
- spelling
- could be/no way
- read sentences – vocabulary development
- auditory discrimination from word list

Lesson 100

Review vowel plus **r**: **ar**

- picture/sound identification
- spelling
- sentence completion
- sentence/picture match – identify **ar**
- puzzle/make-believe words and phrases
- auditory discrimination from word list
- read sentences – vocabulary development

Lesson 101

Review vowel plus **r**: **or**

- picture/sound identification
- spelling
- sentence completion
- alphabetical order
- yes/no choice
- read sentences – vocabulary development
- crossword puzzle

Lesson 102

Vowel plus **r**: **er, ir, ur**

- rule for vowel plus **r**: **er, ir, ur**
- sound identification from written word
- printing
- picture/sentence match – **er** sound identi-fication
- puzzle/make-believe words and phrases
- read sentences – vocabulary development
- could be/no way

Lesson 103

Vowel plus **r**: **ir**

- review rule for vowel plus **r**: **ir**
- sound identification from written word
- printing
- picture/sentence match – **ir** sound identification
- puzzle/make-believe words and phrases
- read sentences – vocabulary development
- auditory discrimination

Lesson 104

Vowel plus **r**: **ur**

- review rule for vowel plus **r**: **ur**
- printing
- picture/sentence match – **ur** sound identification
- puzzle/make-believe words and phrases
- read sentences – vocabulary development
- sound identification

Lesson 105

Review vowel plus **r**: **er, ir, ur**

- picture/sound association
- sentence completion
- printing
- sentence/picture match – sound identification
- words in column
- rhyming
- auditory discrimination from word list
- could be/no way

Lesson 106

Review vowel plus **r**: **ar, or**

- picture/sound association
- sentence completion
- alphabetical order
- picture/sentence match
- words in columns
- yes/no
- rhyming

Lesson 107

Review all vowels plus **r**

- picture/sound association
- sentence completion
- alphabetical order
- rhyming
- picture/sentence match
- word/picture match

Lesson 108

Plurals – **s**

- rule for plurals – **s**
- singular and plural identification
- spelling
- picture/phrase match
- sentence completion
- pictures – choice of plurals or singular

Lesson 109

Plurals – **es**

- rule for plurals – **es**
- spelling
- picture/phrase match
- sentence completion
- pictures – choice of plurals or singular

Lesson 110

Plurals – **y** into **ies**

- rule for **y** into **ies**
- spelling
- picture – plural identification
- phrase/picture match
- sentence completion
- pictures – choice of plurals or singular

Lesson 111

Review plurals – **s**, **es**, **ies**

- plural identification
- spelling
- word identification with plurals
- sentence/picture match – identify plurals

Lesson 112

Review double vowels – **ee**

- review rule for double vowels – **ee**
- picture/sound identification
- print/diacritical markings
- word/picture match
- rhyming
- puzzle/make-believe words and phrases
- sentence comprehension
- spelling
- alphabetical order

Lesson 113

Review double vowels – **ee**, **oa** – apostrophe

- picture/sound association
- printing – diacritical markings
- sentence completion
- spelling
- rhyming
- rule for apostrophe – possession
- sentence exchange – single possession
- sentence exchange – plural possession

Lesson 114

Review double vowels – **ai**, **ea**

- picture/sound association
- column printing
- sentence completion
- spelling
- review apostrophe rule
- sentence exchange – single possession
- sentence exchange – plural possession

Lesson 115

Review all double vowels

- picture/sound association
- printing – diacritical markings
- sentence completion
- puzzle/make-believe words and phrases
- spelling

Lesson 116

Digraph **ay**

- rule for digraph **ay**
- picture/sound association
- printing
- rhyming
- puzzle/make-believe words and phrases
- sentence comprehension
- spelling
- alphabetical order

Lesson 117

Digraph **ey**

- rule for digraph **ey**
- picture/sound association
- printing – diacritical marking
- read sentences – vocabulary development
- rhyming
- puzzle/make-believe words and phrases
- alphabetical order

Lesson 118

Review digraphs **ay**, **ey** – apostrophe

- review digraph rule – **ay**, **ey**
- word/sound association
- sentence completion
- picture/word match
- spelling
- review apostrophe rule
- print sentence exchange for single possession
- print sentence exchange for plural possession

Lesson 119

Diphthong **ow**

- rule for diphthong **ow**
- word/sound association
- picture/word match
- sentence completion
- auditory determination from word list
- printing from copy

Lesson 120

Diphthong **ou**

- rule for both sounds of **ou**
- picture/sound association
- sentence completion
- printing sentences from copy – identify punctuation

Lesson 121

Review digraphs **ay**, **ey**

- picture/sound association
- word/picture match
- spelling
- sentence completion
- noun identification
- sentence sequence
- alphabetical order
- picture/sentence match – **ay**, **ey** identified
- auditory discrimination from word list
- make-believe sentences

Lesson 122

Review digraphs **ay**, **ey**; diphthongs **ow**, **ou**

- picture/word association
- spelling
- sentence completion
- word/picture match – sound identification
- auditory discrimination from word bank
- make-believe phrase

Lesson 123

Digraphs **aw**, **au** – proper nouns – creative writing

- rule for digraphs **aw**, **au**
- picture/sound association
- picture/word match
- word/sound association
- spelling
- sentence completion
- printing – punctuation
- creative writing

- sentence printing – proper nouns
- make-believe phrase

Lesson 124

Digraph **ew**

- rule for digraph **ew**
- picture/sound association
- picture/word match
- spelling
- sentence completion
- review proper nouns
- rule for common noun
- common nouns in sentences
- printing sentences – quotation marks
- auditory discrimination
- make-believe phrase

Lesson 125

Diphthong **oy**

- rule for diphthong **oy**
- picture/sound association
- spelling
- word/picture match
- sentence completion
- proper and common noun identification
- quotation marks
- alphabetical order
- printing
- auditory discrimination from word list

Lesson 126

Review digraphs **aw**, **au**, **ew**; diphthong **oy**

- picture/sound association
- picture/word match
- auditory discrimination from word list
- sentence completion
- printing
- rhyming

Lesson 127

Diphthong **oi**

- rule for diphthong **oi**
- picture/sound association
- picture/word match

- printing
- sentences – sound identification
- make-believe phrases
- spelling
- sentences – vocabulary development
- printing – punctuation

Lesson 128

Review diphthongs **ow**, **ou**; digraphs **ay**, **ey**

- picture/sound association
- sentence completion
- alphabetical order
- rhyming
- sentence/picture match
- printing – punctuation
- auditory discrimination from word list

Lesson 129

Review digraphs **aw**, **au**, **ew**

- picture/sound association
- sentence completion
- picture/word match
- sentences – quotation marks
- auditory discrimination from word list
- spelling
- make-believe phrases

Lesson 130

Review **ow**, **ou**

- picture/sound association
- picture/word match
- spelling
- sentences – sound discrimination
- make-believe phrase
- sentences – punctuation
- auditory discrimination from word list

Lesson 131

Review diphthongs **oy**, **oi**

- picture/sound association
- picture/word match
- spelling
- auditory discrimination from word list
- sentences – sound discrimination

- sentence/picture match
- rhyming
- printing/punctuation

Lesson 132

Letter **y** as in **cry**

- rule for letter **y** as in **cry**
- picture/sound association
- spelling
- word/picture match
- read sentences – vocabulary development
- rhyming
- sentence completion
- auditory discrimination from word list
- printing

Lesson 133

Letter **y** as in **baby**

- rule for Letter **y** as in **baby**
- picture/sound association
- spelling
- word/picture match
- read sentences – vocabulary development
- rhyming
- sentence completion
- auditory discrimination from word list
- printing sentence

Lesson 134

Review Letter **y** as in **cry**, **baby**

- review letter **y** sounds
- picture/sound association
- column printing
- sentence completion
- capitalization – proper nouns
- spelling
- auditory discrimination from word list

Lesson 135

Vowel digraph – special **oo** as in **book**

- rule for vowel digraph – **oo** as in **book**
- picture/printing

- read sentences/sound association
- printing
- auditory discrimination from word list
- rhyming
- read sentences – vocabulary development

Lesson 136

Vowel digraph – special **oo** as in **tooth**

- Rule for vowel digraph – special **oo** as in **tooth**
- picture/printing
- read sentences/sound association
- printing
- auditory discrimination from word list
- rhyming
- read sentences – vocabulary development
- printing sentence from copy

Lesson 137

Review all digraphs/diphthongs

- spelling
- sentence/picture match
- common nouns

Lesson 138

Review letter **y** – long **i** and **e**

- spelling
- sentence completion
- rhyming
- auditory discrimination from word list

Lesson 139

Silent letter **w**

- rule for silent **w**
- picture/word association
- spelling
- printing
- sentences/word identification
- auditory discrimination from word list
- picture description
- make-believe phrase

Lesson 140

Silent letter **k**

- rule for silent **k**
- picture/word association
- spelling
- printing
- make-believe phrase
- auditory discrimination
- sentences – word identification
- picture description

Lesson 141

Silent letter **b**

- rule for silent **b**
- picture/word association
- spelling
- printing
- make-believe phrase
- auditory discrimination from word list
- sentences – word identification
- word discrimination

Lesson 142

Review silent letters **b**, **k**, **w**

- word identification
- word/picture match
- spelling
- auditory discrimination from word list
- sentence/picture match
- identify silent letters
- letter writing

Lesson 143

Silent letter **g**

- rule for silent **g**
- printing
- spelling
- word discrimination
- sentence/picture match
- auditory discrimination from word list
- spelling
- picture description
- questions

Lesson 144

Silent **gh**

- rule for silent **gh**
- word/picture association
- spelling
- phrase match
- auditory discrimination from word list
- sentence/picture match
- puzzle picture

Lesson 145

Review silent letters – **w**, **k**, **b**, **gn**, **gh**

- word/picture identification
- column printing
- auditory discrimination from word list
- word identification
- story comprehension
- creative sentence writing

Lesson 146

le endings

- rule for words ending in le
- word/picture identification
- printing
- word/picture match
- sentence/word identification
- make-believe phrase
- sentence completion
- story comprehension

Lesson 147

Words with **all**

- rule for words with **all**
- word/picture association
- printing
- word/picture match
- spelling
- sentence/word identification
- make-believe phrases
- sentence/comprehension
- story comprehension
- creative sentence writing

Lesson 148

Syllables – double consonants
- rule for double consonants
- word/picture identification
- printing
- sentence/word discrimination

Lesson 149

Syllables – compound words
- rule for syllables with compound words
- word/picture identification
- printing compound words
- word-parts match
- sentences word identification
- make-believe phrase
- word identification
- compound word identification

Lesson 150

Syllables – consonant between vowels
- rule for syllables
- syllable recognition
- printing
- sentences/syllable recognition
- auditory discrimination from word list
- make-believe phrases
- sentences – punctuation
- picture sequence

Lesson 151

Review syllables
- compound word identification
- word/picture match
- sentence completion
- creative sentences using compound words
- creative sentences using double consonants

Lesson 152

Suffix **ing** – prepositions
- signal for word ending with ing
- word/picture match
- spelling

- sentence completion – base word
- rule for prepositions
- picture/identify prepositional phrases

Lesson 153

Special soft **c**
- rule for soft **c**
- reading/printing
- word/picture match
- spelling
- sentences/word identification
- sentence completion
- review noun rule
- identify nouns in sentences
- creative writing of nouns

Lesson 154

Special soft **g**
- rule for soft **g**
- reading/printing
- word/picture match
- spelling
- column printing
- alphabetical order
- make-believe phrases
- sentences/word identification
- picture sequence

Lesson 155

Review ending **ing**, soft **c**, soft **g**
- base word completion
- sentence completion
- picture/word choice
- sentence completion
- sentence sequence
- creative sentence

Lesson 156

Non-phonetic **alk**, **ph** – contractions
- rule for **ph**
- picture/word identification
- printing
- word/picture match

- spelling
- sentence completion
- rule for words with **alk**
- picture/word
- read sentences/vocabulary development
- rule for contractions
- words for contractions
- creative use of contractions

Lesson 157

Non-phonetic **old**, **ost**, **olt**

- rule for non-phonetic word parts – **old**, **ost**, **olt**
- picture/word identification
- printing
- word/picture match
- read sentences/vocabulary development
- action verbs
- sentence completion
- sentence/picture match – action verb identified
- creative action verb

Lesson 158

Non-phonetic **ild**, **ind**

- rule for non-phonetic word parts – **ild**, **ind**
- picture/word identification
- printing
- spelling
- sentence completion
- nouns: proper, common
- pronouns
- verbs
- creative sentences

Lesson 159

Review non-phonetic word parts – **alk**, **old**, **ost**, **olt**, **ind**, **ild**

- picture/word match
- printing
- spelling
- picture/word completion choice
- sentence completion
- crossword puzzle
- auditory discrimination

Lesson 160

Review all

- spelling
- plurals
- double vowels
- silent **e**
- picture/word match
- diacritical markings
- double consonants
- syllables
- compound words
- soft **c** and **g**
- picture/word match

Teacher's Lessons

Lesson 1 - Short a

Overview:

- Introduce the alphabet through the Alphabet Story
- Use child's name to emphasize the importance of letters in forming words
- Learn to follow directions for marking pictures
- Introduce the letter **a**—its name, sound, and shape—through pictures
- Identify words that begin with the sound of **a**
- Print both capital and lowercase **a**

Materials and Supplies:

- Teacher's Guide & Student Workbook
- Alphabet Story
- Alphabet Poem
- White board
- Alphabet flow chart
- Reader 1: *Ann's Cat*

Teaching Tips:

Introduce and demonstrate the words **top**, **bottom**, **left**, **right**, **circle** and **x**; paper **top to bottom**, **left to right**.

Emphasize auditory skills for correct reproduction of letter sounds. Identify child's hand preference, proper position of holding a pencil, and proper position of holding hands on the paper.

Introduction to Workbook Activities:

Read the alphabet story (see the Table of Contents for the page number) and explain the need for letters to make words. Explain how letters are used to make names. The alphabet is necessary in learning to read.

Read the alphabet poem and display the illustration that goes with each letter.

Each day recite the alphabet through all 26 letters. The emphasis is on the letter name rather than sequence. Recognition of both capital and lowercase letters is more important at this time.

Discuss **Rule I**: Every word must have a vowel in it. Discuss **Rule 2**: If there is only one vowel in a word, it is usually used as a short-vowel sound. Teach the letter **a**—the recognition of the letter, its name, its sound, and its printed form. Study the pictures used to identify the short sound of the letter **a**.

Pictures: **apple, add, alligator, astronaut, anteater**

Emphasize the short **a** sound, and have the child imitate as a single sound and as it is used at the beginning of each of the picture words.

Lines on the board should be noted as **top**, **middle**, and **bottom**. Point out the starting and ending lines for the letter **a**.

Activity 1. Do these activities together. Have the student recognize the pictures and repeat so the beginning sound is distinct. Student will put a circle around the pictures that start with the sound of **a**.

Pictures: **ant, ax, Ann, camel fan, anteater, apple, fox**

Activity 2. Student is to identify the short **a** sound in the MIDDLE of the word.

Pictures: **Max, fan, bat, mad**

Activity 3. Student will underline the short **a** in the middle of the word. Say the sound of short **a**. Refer to original words if necessary for comparison.

Pictures: **bat, dad, pan, ran**

Activities 4 & 5. Review the letters of the alphabet. Begin printing of capital **A**. Use the board for demonstration of all printing. Have the student note beginning strokes and each additional stroke. They need to be aware of the letter's placement on the lines.

Activity 6. Begin printing of lowercase **a**.

Activity 7. Identify the difference between the capital **A** and lowercase **a**.

Activity 8. Practice in printing capital and lowercase **a**.

Activity 9. Print an **a** under the pictures that start with the sound of **a**.

Pictures: **ant, anteater, alligator, bear ax, fox, dog, astronaut**

Activity 10. Creative drawing using words with short **a**. Directions are to print the letter and color specific parts.

Color words: **black**, **red**

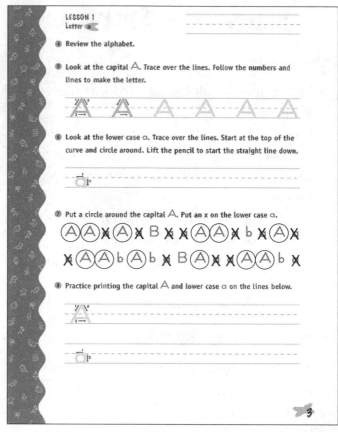

Lesson 2 - Letter b

Overview:

- Reread Alphabet Story
- Recite the alphabet through all 26 letters
- Introduce consonant **b** and teach the sound
- Identify words that start with sound of **b**
- Teach both capital and lowercase **b** for printing

Materials and Supplies:

- Teacher's Guide & Student Workbook
- White board
- Alphabet Story
- Alphabet Poem
- Alphabet flow chart
- Reader 1: *The Bug Bag*

Teaching Tips:

Introduce the consonant **b**. Make sure that a vowel does not follow the sound of **b**. It is a quick sound where the lips barely meet. Do not let the sound of **b** become **bu** or **be**.

Introduction to Workbook Activities:

Review the alphabet story and the alphabet poem. Use the illustrations that go with the letters as flashcards. With daily practice the students will be able to recite the sentences and pronounce the words with the correct initial sounds. The students can color copies of the illustrations for additional reinforcement.

Introduce the consonant **b**—its name, sound, and shape. Do all of these activities together. Have the student recognize the pictures and repeat the word so the beginning sound is distinct.

Pictures: **ball, bathtub, Bible, bat, bottle, bag**

Activity 1. Student is to recognize the pictures and repeat the words so the beginning sound is distinct. Student will put a circle around the pictures that start with the sound of **b**.

Pictures: **bee, ball, bike, belt bib, basket, bed, bell**

Activity 2. Combine **b** with short **a** sound. Underline the **ba** sound for each picture.

Pictures: **bat, bag, band, bank**

Activity 3. Student is to identify the sound of **b** at the end of each picture word.

Pictures: **bathtub, cab, horse, box**

Activities 4 & 5. Review the alphabet. Begin printing of capital **B**. Use the board for demonstration of all printing. Have the student note beginning strokes and each additional stroke. They need to be aware of the letter's placement on the lines.

Activity 6. Begin printing lowercase **b**. Emphasize the need for starting both capital and lowercase with the straight line down first.

Activity 7. Distinguish between capital and lowercase **b**. Circle the capital **B**. Put an **X** on the lowercase **b**. Ignore the letter **a**.

Activity 8. Practice printing capital and lowercase **b**.

Activity 9. Do the activities together. Have the student recognize the pictures and become aware of the sound of **ba**. Print **ba** under the appropriate pictures.

   Pictures: **basket, bat, ax, bag band, boat, boy, bath**

Activity 10. Creative drawing to use the letter **b**. Follow directions in printing capital and lowercase **b**.

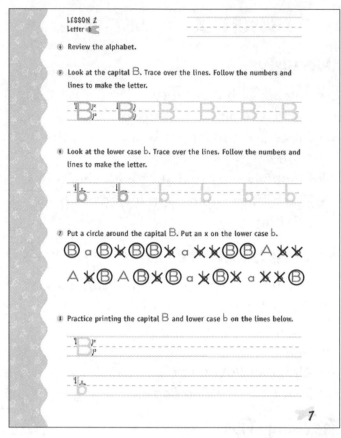

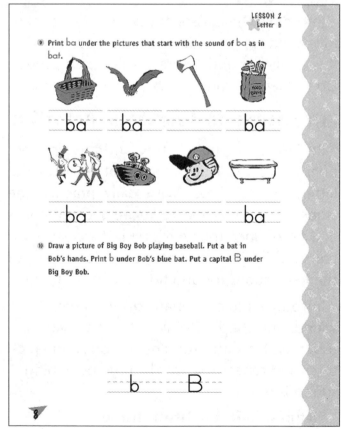

Lesson 3 - Letter d

Overview:

- Review consonant **b** and vowel **a**
- Introduce the consonant **d**
- Teach recognition of capital and lower-case **d**
- Teach the beginning sound of **da**

Materials and Supplies:

- Teacher's Guide & Student Workbook
- White board
- Alphabet Story
- Alphabet Poem
- Alphabet flow chart
- Reader 1: *Dad's Cat*

Teaching Tips:

Introduce the consonant **d**. Encourage students to blend the consonant and the short vowel together quickly instead of continuing to sound out each letter separately. Teach the printing of the letter **d** with the half circle first, then adding the straight line as the second stroke. This eliminates the reversal of **d** and **b**.

Introduction to Workbook Activities:

Review the alphabet story and the alphabet poem. Use the illustrations that go with the letters as flashcards. With daily practice the students will be able to recite the sentences and pronounce the words with the correct initial sounds. The students can color copies of the illustrations for additional reinforcement.

Introduce the consonant **d**—its name, sound, and shape. Do all of these activities together. Have the student recognize the pictures and repeat the words so the beginning sound is distinct.

Pictures: **dad, dog, desert, doll, desk**

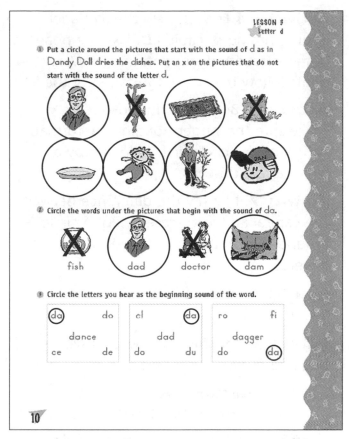

Activity 1. Student is to recognize each picture and repeat it so the beginning sound is distinct. Student will put a circle around the pictures that start with the sound of **d** and an **X** over those that do not.

Pictures: **dad, monkey, dollar, cake dish, doll, dig, Dan**

Activity 2. Teach blending of consonants with vowels. Review the rule: ONE VOWEL IN A WORD USUALLY HAS THE SHORT SOUND. Do this activity together. Emphasize the sound **da** at the beginning of the word.

Pictures: **fish, dad, doctor, dam**

Activity 3. The student will listen for the words that begin with **da**. Overemphasize the sound of **da**. Student will have a choice of three other double letter beginnings. Put a circle around the correct one.

Words: **dance, dad, dagger**

Activities 4 & 5. Review the alphabet. Begin printing of capital **D**. Use the board for demonstration of all printing. Have the students follow the stroke formation of the letter.

Activity 6. Begin printing lowercase **d**. Make sure the student begins the formation with a partial circle first, followed by a straight line down.

Activity 7. Identify the difference between the capital and lowercase **d**. Put a circle around the capital **D**. Put an **X** on the lowercase **d**.

Activity 8. Practice in printing capital and lowercase **d**.

Activity 9. Identify pictures and words beginning with the sound of **d**.

   Pictures: **doctor, bus, dog, ant desk, add, dentist, dad**

Activity 10. Identify the sound of **da**. Print **da** on the lines where appropriate.

   Pictures: **dam, duck, damp, Dan**

Activity 11. Student will count the number of sets of the combined sound of **da**.

Activity 12. Creative discussion of words that begin with the sound of **d**.

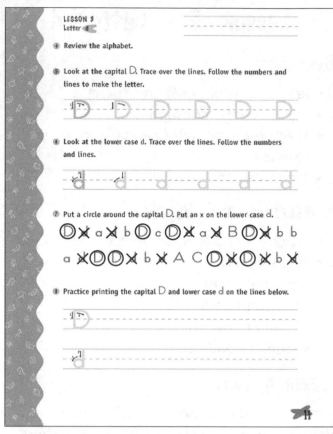

Lesson 4 - Short o

Overview:

- Review alphabet and the importance of letters in the formation of words
- Review the rule of having one vowel in a word, and if only one, it makes a short vowel sound
- Introduce the vowel **o**—its name, sound, and shape through pictures
- Teach printing of capital and lowercase **o**
- Identify words starting with the short **o** sound
- Identify words with the short **o** in the middle
- Identify words that start with the sounds of **lo**

Materials and Supplies:

- Teacher's Guide & Student Workbook
- White board
- Alphabet Story
- Alphabet Poem
- Alphabet flow chart
- Reader 1: *Don's Big Dog*

Teaching Tips:

Remember to identify each new letter as a consonant or a vowel as it is introduced. In using the alphabet flow chart, introduce the Vowel Family. Take time for the student to hear the short **o** sound at the beginning and middle of the word. Emphasize that each word must have a vowel.

Introduction to Workbook Activities:

Review the alphabet story and the alphabet poem. Use the illustrations that go with the letters as flashcards. With daily practice the students will be able to recite the sentences and pronounce the words with the correct initial sounds. The students can color copies of the illustrations for additional reinforcement.

Introduce the vowel **o**—its name, sound, and shape. Have the student recognize the pictures and repeat the word so the beginning sound is distinct.

Pictures: **olive, octopus, ostrich, otter, ox**

Activity 1. Student is to recognize each picture and repeat the word so the beginning sound is distinct. Student will put a circle around the pictures that start with the vowel sound of **o**.

Pictures: **ostrich, off, olive, legs octopus, ox, mouse, otter**

Activity 2. Do these activities together. Student is to identify the short **o** in the MIDDLE of the word.

Pictures: **ducks, log, box, Bob, hog, doll, cob, dog**

Activities 3 & 4. Review the alphabet. Review the vowel sound of **o**. Begin printing of capital and lowercase **o**. Use the board for demonstration of all printing. Have the student note the way the circle is formed, starting from the top right. They need to be aware of the letter's placement between the lines for both capital and lowercase.

Activity 5. Print **o** under the pictures that START with the short sound of **o**.

Pictures: **otter, ostrich, tree, octopus fish, olive, bucket, ox**

Activity 6. Combine **l** with short **o**. Review short vowel rule. Circle the letters that make the sound of **lo** in each word below.

Words: **map, log, lock, long**

Activity 7. Teacher and student must work together to identify the pictures. Put a circle around the short **o** in the MIDDLE of the word.

Pictures: **frog, lock, camel, dog hot, dig, top, jog**

Activity 8. Practice printing letters **ba**.

Activity 9. Practice printing the consonant before the vowel – **bo** and **do**.

Activity 10. Practice printing the word **dad**.

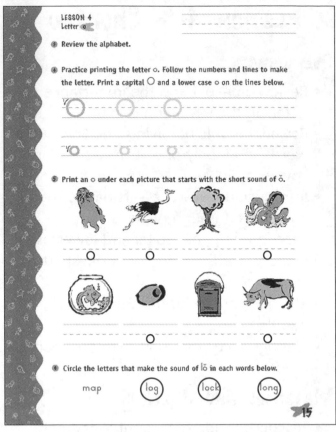

Lesson 5 - Letter c

Overview:

- Review the entire alphabet using the alphabet flow chart
- Review the names and sounds for the alphabet letters: **a**, **b**, **d**, **o**
- Introduce the consonant **c**. With all the letters, emphasize the words **consonant** or **vowel**
- Teach the letter **c**—its name, sound, and shape
- Review Phonics Rules of vowels
- Identify words that begin with **c**, **ca**, **co**

Materials and Supplies:

- Teacher's Guide & Student Workbook
- White board
- Alphabet Story
- Alphabet Poem
- Reader 1: *Cal's Cap*

Teaching Tips:

Continue emphasizing the importance of the letters in the alphabet. Create excitement with the recognition of beginning reading.

Introduction to Workbook Activities:

Review the alphabet story and the alphabet poem. Use the illustrations that go with the letters as flashcards. With daily practice the students will be able to recite the sentences and pronounce the words with the correct initial sounds. The students can color copies of the illustrations for additional reinforcement.

Introduce the consonant **c**—its name, sound, and shape. Student must recognize the pictures and repeat the word so the beginning sound is distinct. Have the students think of other things that begin with the sound of **c**.

Pictures: **cake, cup, cat, cap, candle, candy**

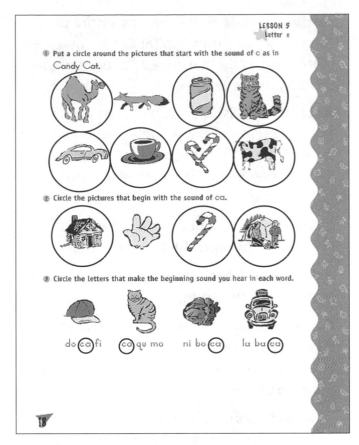

Activity 1. Student is to recognize the pictures and repeat the words so the beginning sound is distinct. Student will put a circle around the pictures that start with the sound of **c**.

Pictures: **camel, fox, can, cat car, cup, candy, cow**

Activity 2. Combine **c** with short **a** sound. Circle the pictures that begin with the sound of **ca**.

Pictures: **cabin, hand, candy, camp**

Activity 3. Identification of beginning consonant **c** combined with vowel **a**.

Pictures: **cap, cat, cabbage, cab**

Activities 4 & 5. Review the entire alphabet, then begin printing capital **C** and lowercase **c**. Note should be taken as to placement and spacing of the letter **c**.

Activity 6. Distinguish between capital **C** and lowercase **c**. Put a circle around the capital **C**. Put an **X** on the lowercase **c**.
Say the names of the other letters but do not mark them.

Activity 7. Identification of sound **ca**. Put a circle around the letter groups.

Activity 8. Count the number of sets of letters making the sound of **ca**.

Activity 9. Do the activities together. Have the student recognize the pictures and become aware of the sound **co**. Have student print **co** under the appropriate pictures.

    Pictures: **cob, cabbage, cod, collar, cot, cup, cop, cotton**

All activities including sounding of letters must be done together. Review the Vowel Rule. Have student print the beginning consonant **c** and vowel **a** under each appropriate picture.

    Pictures: **cab, calf, bat, can, cup, fan, camel, cabbage**

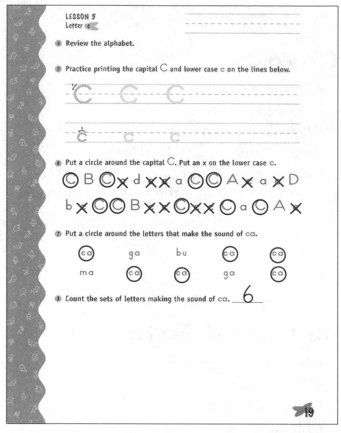

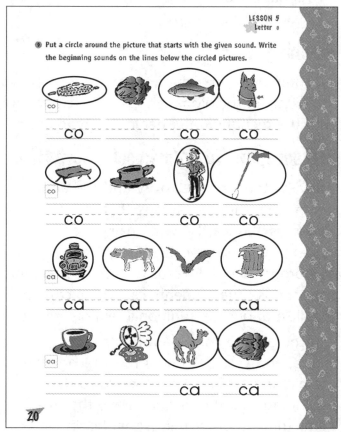

Lesson 6 - Short Vowel e

Overview:

- Review the names and sounds for the alphabet letters: **a**, **b**, **d**, **o**, **c**
- Introduce vowel **e**
- Teach recognition of capital **E** and lowercase **e**
- Recognize duplicate words for matching.
- Identify beginning consonant sounds of words with short **a**, **o**, **e**
- Introduce made-up funny phrases

Materials and Supplies:

- Teacher's Guide & Student Workbook
- White board
- Alphabet Story
- Alphabet Poem
- Alphabet flow chart
- Reader 1: *Ben*

Teaching Tips:

Continue reciting the alphabet using the flow chart. Point out where the individual letters are arranged in the alphabet. Always follow the same steps in introducing a new letter.

Introduction to Workbook Activities:

Review the alphabet story and the alphabet poem. Use the illustrations that go with the letters as flashcards. With daily practice the students will be able to recite the sentences and pronounce the words with the correct initial sounds. The students can color copies of the illustrations for additional reinforcement.

Review the Short Vowel Rule. Reinforce the value of vowels in a word. Again, do all of the activities together. Have the student recognize the pictures and repeat them, emphasizing the **e** sound.

Pictures: **elk, engine, Ed, elbow, elephant**

Activity 1. Student is to recognize the pictures and repeat the words so the beginning sound is distinct. Student will put a circle around the pictures that start with the vowel sound **e**.

Pictures: **football, Ed, elephant, envelope, elk, ostrich, elbow, engine**

Activity 2. Review the vowel sound **e**. Note that some of the pictures may have a different vowel sound than the short **e**. Circle the words under the pictures that have a short **e** sound in the MIDDLE of the word.

Pictures: **desk, bed, hat, den**

Activity 3. Student must realize that all of the phrases or sentences are made up for fun reading. Read the funny phrase and enjoy the humor.

Activity 4. Student is to recognize the pictures and repeat the words so the beginning sound is distinct. Student will circle the picture starting with the sound of **de**.

Pictures: **den, dentist, lamb, elephant, dish, desk, cat, desert**

Activity 5. Student is to recognize the pictures and repeat the words so the beginning sound is distinct.

Pictures: **Beth, doll, mad, bed Ben, legs, belt, beg**

Activity 6. Student is to identify identical words in each square. Draw a line from the words that match.

Words: **dad, Ed, elephant, bed tent, Ted, cot, dot**

Activities 7 & 8. Review the alphabet, then begin printing capital **E** and lowercase **e**. Note should be taken as to placement and spacing of the letter **e**.

Activity 9. Identify the letter **e** at the beginning of the word. Print **e** under each picture that starts with the short vowel sound **e**.

Pictures: **elephant, Ed, can, engine**

Activity 10. Review the vowel sound **e**. Note that some of the pictures will have different vowel sounds than the short **e**. Student is to circle the pictures that have the sound of short **e** in the MIDDLE of the word.

Pictures: **bed, Ben, fan, pen**

Activity 11. Practice writing the first consonant and adding a short **e** to **be** and **de**.

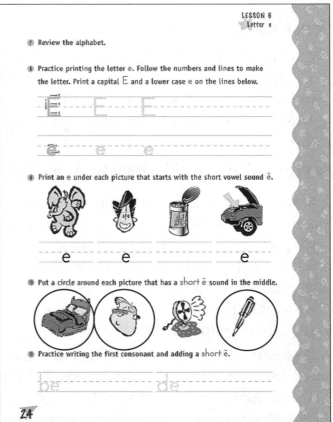

52   *Horizons Kindergarten Phonics and Reading*

Lesson 7 - Letter f

Overview:

- Review the names and sounds for the alphabet letters: **a, b, d, o, c, e**
- Review the Vowel Rules
- Introduce the letter **f**—its name, sound, and shape through pictures

Materials and Supplies:

- Teacher's Guide & Student Workbook
- White board
- Alphabet Story
- Alphabet Poem
- Alphabet flow chart
- Flashcards
- Reader 1: *The Fox*

Teaching Tips:

Use Alphabet flashcards to review the letters taught in the previous lessons. Encourage the student to print on the board from dictation. Encourage them to print from memory each of the previous letters. Encourage them to add a vowel to a beginning consonant. Have them make the sounds they have written. Make it a game to have the student print one letter and the teacher adds another to create a beginning sound. When learning to sound the letter **f**, encourage the student to place the top teeth just over the lower lip and use a breath to form the sound. The sound of **f** is soft and voiceless.

Introduction to Workbook Activities:

Review the alphabet story and the alphabet poem. Use the illustrations that go with the letters as flashcards. With daily practice the students will be able to recite the sentences and pronounce the words with the correct initial sounds. The students can color copies of the illustrations for additional reinforcement.

Introduce the consonant **f**. Review the names and sounds for the letters previously

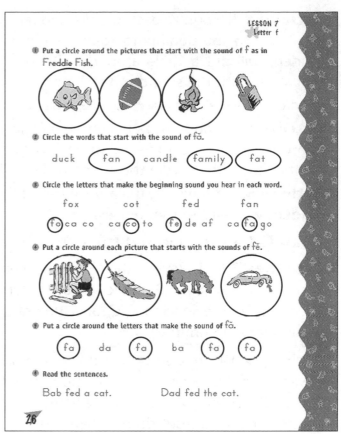

learned. Have the student recognize the pictures and repeat the word so the beginning sound is distinct. Study the pictures used to identify the consonant sound of **f**. Have the student think of other things that begin with the sound of **f**.

Pictures: **family, fish, frog, fork, fan, feather, fox**

Activity 1. Student is to recognize each picture and repeat the word so the beginning sound is distinct. Student will circle the pictures starting with the consonant **f**.

Pictures: **fish, football, fire, lock**

Activity 2. Direct the student how to look at the beginning of a word and determine its sound. Student is to circle the words that START with the sound of **fa**.

Words: **duck, fan, candle, family, fat**

Activity 3. Student has the choice of three consonant/vowel beginnings. Student is to circle the letters that make the BEGINNING SOUNDS you hear in each word.

Words: **fox, cot, fed, fan**

Activity 4. Recognize each picture and repeat the word so the beginning sound is distinct. Student will put a circle around each picture that starts with the sound of **fe**.

Picture: **fence, feather, horse, fender**

Activity 5. Distinguish between beginning consonants plus the vowel **a**. Student will circle the letters that make the sound of **fa**.

Activity 6. Sight words: the **a** must be taught. Student will read the sentences.

Bab fed a cat. Dad fed the cat.

Activities 7 & 8. Review the alphabet, then begin printing capital **F** and lowercase letter **f**. Emphasize the spacing and formation of the letter when printing.

Activity 9. Distinguish between capital **F** and lowercase **f**. Put a circle around the capital **F**. Put an **X** on the lowercase **f**. Read the other letters in between, but do not mark them.

Activity 10. Circle the words below the pictures that START with the consonant **f**.

Pictures: **frog, fiddle, fork, ducks**

Activity 11. Discuss making up words when the first alphabet was being formed. Talk about sliding letters together to make words. Make a game out of sounding out make-up words. Practice printing on the white board first. Then have the student print the make-up word after he has learned to pronounce it. At this time the teacher can determine if further drill is required.

Make-up Words: **feb, fab, fef, fof**

Activity 12. Identify the pictures and words. Discuss the sound of the FIRST consonant plus a vowel. Print the first consonant and vowel on the lines.

Pictures: **fat, fan, fad, fender**

Activity 13. Discuss the puzzle sentences and the fun in reading. Student will trace and then print the puzzle sentence on the lines below.

Puzzle Sentence: **Ed fed a bed.**

54

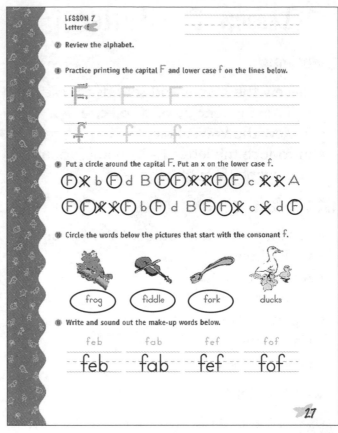

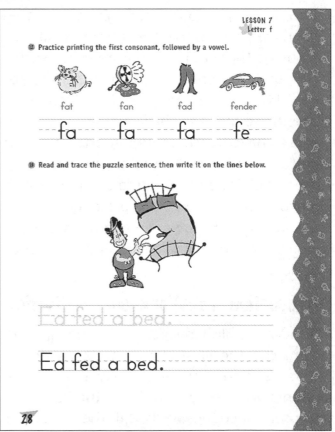

Lesson 8 - Letter g

Overview:

- Review consonants: **b**, **d**, **c**, **f**
- Review vowels and Vowel Rule: **a**, **o**, **e**
- Introduce the consonant **g**—its name, sound, and shape through pictures

Materials and Supplies:

- Teacher's Guide & Student Workbook
- White board
- Alphabet Story
- Alphabet Poem
- Alphabet flow chart
- Flashcards
- Reader 1: *The Van*

Teaching Tips:

Use the alphabet flow chart and flashcards as a tool for review. Have the student select certain letters from a stack, say the sound of the letter, and then print it on the white board. Continue review by picking out a vowel card and two consonants cards to make a real or make-up word. Help the student decide if it is a real word.

Introduction to Workbook Activities:

Review the alphabet story and the alphabet poem. Use the illustrations that go with the letters as flashcards. With daily practice the students will be able to recite the sentences and pronounce the words with the correct initial sounds. The students can color copies of the illustrations for additional reinforcement.

Review the alphabet. Introduce the letter **g**—the name, sound, and shape. The hard sound is the only **g** taught in this lesson. Demonstrate on the white board the formation of the letter **g** with the tail below the line and under the circle of the **g**. Have the student recognize the pictures and repeat the word so the beginning sound is distinct.

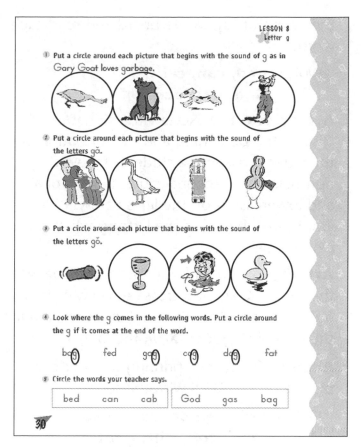

Pictures: **goose, gift, goat, gorilla, gate**

Activity 1. Identify the pictures so the sound of g is distinct. Student will circle the pictures that START with the sound of **g**.

Pictures: **goose, gorilla, dog, golf**

Activity 2. Use the white board to demonstrate the beginning sound of **ga**. Have the student put a circle around each picture that STARTS with the sound of the letters **ga**.

Pictures: **gang, gander, gas, wig**

Activity 3. Have the student put a circle around each picture that STARTS with the sound of the letters **go**.

Pictures: **log, goblet, goggles, gosling**

Activity 4. Discuss the placement of the letter **g** in the following words. Read the words. Put a circle around the **g** if it comes at the END of the word.

Words: **bag, fed, gag, cog, dog, fat**

Activity 5. Read one word from each of the boxes. Student is to circle the correct word then print on the white board and read each word.

Words: **bed, can, cab**
God, gas, bag

Activities 6 & 7. Review the alphabet. Discuss the beginning and the formation of the letter **g**. Have the students follow the numbers for directional clues. Print capital **G** and lowercase **g** on the lines below. Emphasize the tail of the letter **g** which extends below the line.

Activity 8. Student will distinguish between the capital **G** and lowercase **g**. He will also recognize letters other than **g**. Put a circle around the capital **G**. Put an **X** on the lowercase **g**.

Activity 9. Practice printing g under each picture that STARTS with the sound of g.

Pictures: **girl, game, gate, boat**
cat, golf, gift, goat

Activity 10. Discuss the pictures with the student. Identify the pictures and be aware of the vowel sound following the **g**. Practice printing the letter **g** followed by a vowel.

Pictures: **gander, gas, gift, girl**

Activity 11. Use the white board to print the make-up words first. Have the student sound out, read, and then write each make-up word.

Make-up Words: **gac, gaf, dag, gat**

Activity 12. Read the puzzle sentence and write it on the lines below.

Sentence: **Dad fed an egg.**

Lesson 9 - Letter i

Overview:

- Review consonants and vowels
- Introduce the letter **i**
- Use of the letter **I** as a word
- Use of the lowercase letter **i** at the beginning and middle of a word

Materials and Supplies:

- Teacher's Guide & Student Workbook
- White board
- Alphabet Story
- Alphabet Poem
- Alphabet flow chart
- Flashcards
- Reader 1: *The Twins*

Teaching Tips:

Care must be taken to distinguish between the sound of **i** and **e**. Review the alphabet. Introduce the letter **i**—the name, sound, and shape. Also mention that the capital **I** can be used as a word. Demonstrate on the white board the formation of the letter **i** in both capital and lowercase form. Note that the dot is the second stroke on the lowercase **i**. Have the student recognize the pictures and repeat the word so the beginning sound is distinct.

Pictures: **inchworm, ill, iguana, igloo, insect**

Introduction to Workbook Activities:

Review the alphabet story and the alphabet poem. Use the illustrations that go with the letters as flashcards. With daily practice the students will be able to recite the sentences and pronounce the words with the correct initial sounds. The students can color copies of the illustrations for additional reinforcement.

Review the alphabet. Introduce the letter **i**—the name, sound, and shape. Have the student recognize the pictures and repeat the word so the beginning sound is distinct.

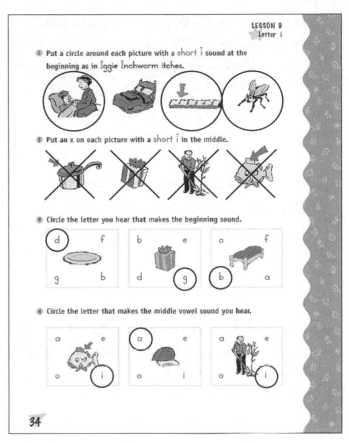

Activity 1. Study the pictures so the student recognizes the beginning sound of **i**. Discuss the meanings of all the pictures. Student will circle pictures that begin with the sound of short **i**.

Pictures: **ill, bed, inch, insect**

Activity 2. Study the pictures. Student must be able to hear the short **i** in the middle of the word. Demonstrate on the white board the placement of vowels used in the middle. Have the student put an **X** on the pictures with short **i** in the MIDDLE.

Pictures: **lid, gift, dig, fin**

Activity 3. Identify the pictures within each square. Have the student choose and circle the letter that is at the BEGINNING of the word.

Pictures: **dish, gift, bed**

Activity 4. Identify the pictures within each square. Have the student choose and circle the vowel sound that is in the MIDDLE of the word.

Pictures: **fin, cap, dig**

Horizons Kindergarten Phonics and Reading

Activities 5 & 6. Review the alphabet. Have the student follow the numbers for directional clues. Practice printing the capital **I** and lowercase **i**.

Activity 7. Study the pictures to identify the sound of **i**. Student will print **i** under each picture that STARTS with the vowel sound **i**.

Words: **igloo, iguana, ill, insect**

Activity 8. Discuss the capital **I** used as a word as it stands alone. Student will read the phrases and print them on the lines below. Teach the sight word **do**.

Phrases: **I did   I do**

Activity 9. Use the white board for practice in recognizing beginning sounds. The student will practice printing and saying the letters below. Use short vowel sounds.

ba	be	bi	bo
da	de	di	do
fa	fe	fi	fo
ga	ge	gi	go

Activity 10. Read together with the teacher. Use diacritical markings on the vowels to indicate the short vowel sound. Use flashcards and the white board to demonstrate the beginning consonant, middle vowel and an additional consonant to finish the word.

da	de	di	do	fo
fa	fe	fi	ga	go

Activity 11. Read the words together. Mark each short vowel. Print the words on the white board for review.

Words: **Dan, God, dig, dog, fed rib, fell, fin, bag, Bob**

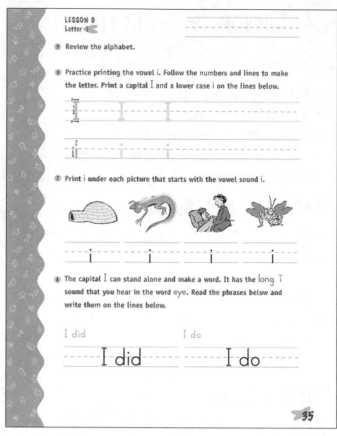

Lesson 10 - Letter h

Overview:

- Review the names and sounds for letters that have been studied
- Review Vowel Rule
- Introduce the consonant **h**—its name, sound, and shape

Materials and Supplies:

- Teacher's Guide & Student Workbook
- White board
- Alphabet Story
- Alphabet Poem
- Alphabet flow chart
- Flashcards
- Reader 1: *Hal Fell*

Teaching Tips:

Review Vowel Rules. When teaching a new letter, be sure the student has a chance to print it on the white board and review its sound.

Introduction to Workbook Activities:

Review the alphabet story and the alphabet poem. Use the illustrations that go with the letters as flashcards. With daily practice the students will be able to recite the sentences and pronounce the words with the correct initial sounds. The students can color copies of the illustrations for additional reinforcement.

Review the alphabet. Introduce the letter **h**—its name, sound, and shape. Have the student identify the pictures and repeat the word so the beginning sound is distinct.

Pictures: **hockey, horn, hog, horse, hat**

Activity 1. Identify the pictures. Student will circle the pictures that START with the **h** sound.

Pictures: **hippo, kitten, heart, house**

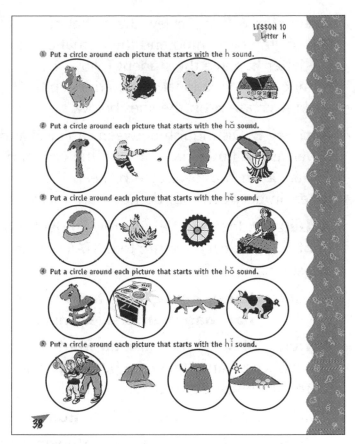

Activity 2. Identify the pictures. Review the vowel sounds that follow a consonant. Have the student put a circle around each picture that STARTS with sound of **ha**.

Pictures: **hammer, hockey, hat, happy**

Activity 3. Identify the pictures. Review the vowel sounds. Have the student put a circle around each picture that STARTS with the sound of **he**.

Pictures: **helmet, hen, wheel, hedge**

Activity 4. Identify the pictures. Review the vowel sounds. Have the student put a circle around each picture that STARTS with the sound of **ho**.

Pictures: **hobbyhorse, hot, fox, hog**

Activity 5. Identify the pictures. Review the vowel sounds. Have the student put a circle around each picture that STARTS with the sound of **hi**.

Pictures: **hit, cap, hip, hill**

Activities 6 & 7. Review the alphabet. Discuss the beginning and the formation of the letter **h**. Have the student follow the numbers for directional clues. Print capital **H** and lowercase **h** on the lines below.

Activity 8. Distinguish between capital **H** and lowercase **h**. Put a circle around the capital **H**. Put an **X** on the lowercase **h**. Read the other letters in between, but do not mark them.

Activity 9. Identify the pictures. Student will print **h** under each picture that STARTS with the sound of **h**.

> Pictures: **hand, horse, dog, house hat, bag, hammer, hamster**

Activity 10. Read the make-up words. Use flashcards and the white board to reinforce the concept of sounding letters.

> Make-up Words: **hab, hef, hib, hom**

Activity 11. Study the pictures. Student is to identify the beginning consonant to complete the spelling word below the pictures. Print the beginning consonant so the spelling words match the pictures.

> Pictures: **dad, hog, bag, bed**

Activity 12. Discuss adding the letter **s** to show the plural form of a word. Student will add **s** at the end of each word to show more than one thing.

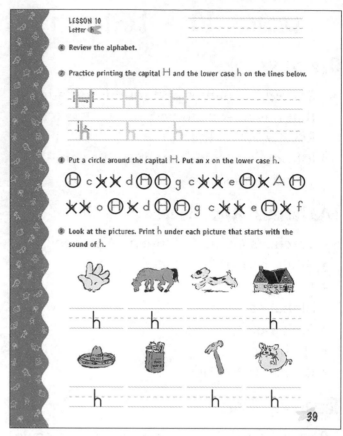

Activity 13. Read the sentences. Have the student trace and then print them on the lines below. Remind the student that the sentence must begin with a capital letter and end with a period. Identify the period (.)

    Sentences: **Ed fed the dog.**
                 Bob had a bed.

Activity 14. Read each puzzle sentence and draw a line to the picture it matches.

    Sentences: **Bob had a hot dog.**
                 Dad hid a hog.
                 Ed fed a cab.

Activity 15. Identify the beginning consonant-vowel or vowel-consonant combination. Print the letters under each picture.

    Pictures: **cab, bad, can, dot,**
              cob, Bob, add, cot

Activity 16. Draw a picture of your home.

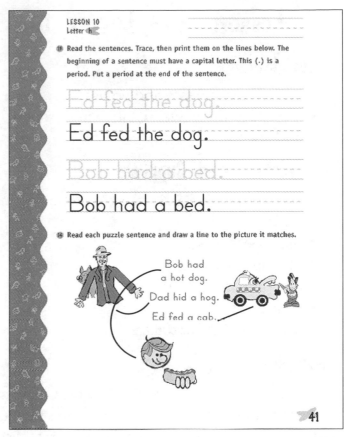

Lesson 11 - Letter u

Overview:

- Review consonants and vowels
- Introduce the vowel **u**—its name, sound, and shape

Materials and Supplies:

- Teacher's Guide & Student Workbook
- White board
- Alphabet Story
- Alphabet Poem
- Alphabet flow chart
- Flashcards
- Reader 1: *Judd and Buzz*

Teaching Tips:

Teach only the short **u**. The long sound of **u** will be taught at a later time. Have the students practice saying the vowel sound **u**. Establish the difference between short **o** and **u**.

Introduction to Workbook Activities:

Review the alphabet story and the alphabet poem. Use the illustrations that go with the letters as flashcards. With daily practice the students will be able to recite the sentences and pronounce the words with the correct initial sounds. The students can color copies of the illustrations for additional reinforcement.

Review the alphabet. Introduce the vowel **u**— its name, sound, and shape. Have the student identify the pictures and repeat the word so the beginning sound is distinct. Review the alphabet. Introduce the vowel **u**. Review the Vowel Rule. Demonstrate on the white board the formation of the capital **U** and lowercase **u** in the placement on the lines. Have the students recognize the pictures and repeat the words so the beginning sound is distinct.

Pictures: **up, usher, umbrella, upside down**

Activity 1. Discuss the pictures and the beginning sound of each. Repeat the words until the short sound of **u** is firmly established. Student will put a circle around each picture that STARTS with a short **u** sound.

Pictures: **usher, under, boat, umbrella**

Activity 2. Discuss the pictures and their meaning. Repeat the words until the short sound of u is firmly established. Student will put a circle around the short **u** sound in the MIDDLE of each word.

Pictures: **rug, puppy, bug, run**

Activity 3. Discuss the pictures and their meaning. Repeat the words until the short sound of u is firmly established. Student will put an **X** on each picture that begins with the sound of **du**.

Pictures: **duck, lamp, dump, bunch**

Activity 4. Discuss the pictures and their meaning. Underline each picture that begins with the sound of **fu**.

Pictures: **fuss, fuzz, fun, gate**

Horizons Kindergarten Phonics and Reading

Activity 5. Establish the vocabulary for every picture. Put a circle around each picture that begins with the sound of **bu**.

Pictures: **button, bug, boots, bun**

Activity 6. Establish the vocabulary for every picture. Underline each picture beginning with the sound of **cu**.

Words: **cut, cup, cop, cuff**

Activity 7. Establish the vocabulary for every picture. Put an **X** over each picture beginning with the sound of **gu**.

Pictures: **gas, gum, gull, dug**

Activity 8. Have student read the words. Put a circle around all the words in the word bank that have the sound of short **u** in the MIDDLE.

Words:

puff	**rug**	**top**	**jug**	**cut**
gull	**sun**	**cob**	**run**	**bud**
bad	**nut**	**bed**	**cuff**	**mud**

Activities 9 & 10. Review the alphabet. Review the vowels on the white board. Student will practice printing the capital **U** and lowercase vowel **u**, following the directional clues.

Activity 11. Study the pictures and discuss the vocabulary. Student will print a **u** under the words that have a short **u** sound.

Pictures: **upside down, cut, mug, umbrella**

Activity 12. Draw a line from the pictures to the matching words.

Pictures: **bud, bag, dug, bug**

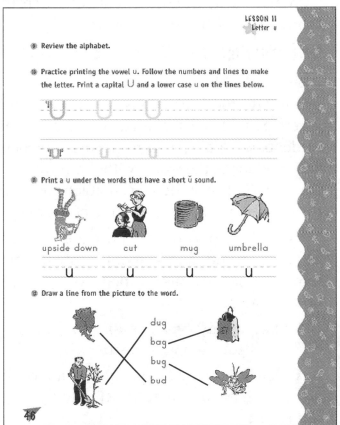

Lesson 12 - Letter t

Overview:

- Review the letters of the alphabet
- Introduce the consonant **t**—its name, sound, and shape
- Practice in combining the letter **t** with all the vowels

Material and Supplies:

- Teacher's Guide & Student Workbook
- White board
- Alphabet Story
- Alphabet Poem
- Alphabet flow chart
- Flashcards
- Reader 1: *A Tooth*

Teaching Tips:

Use flashcards and the alphabet flow chart to review the consonants and vowels

Introduction to Workbook Activities:

Review the alphabet story and the alphabet poem. Use the illustrations that go with the letters as flashcards. With daily practice the students will be able to recite the sentences and pronounce the words with the correct initial sounds. The students can color copies of the illustrations for additional reinforcement.

Review the alphabet. Introduce the letter **t**—its name, sound, and shape. Identify the pictures and practice saying them so the sound of **t** is distinct.

Pictures: **teddy bear, telephone, top, turtle, tiger, tent**

Activity 1. Identify the pictures. Put a circle around the pictures that START with the sound of **t**.

Pictures: **top, puppy, tiger, turtle**

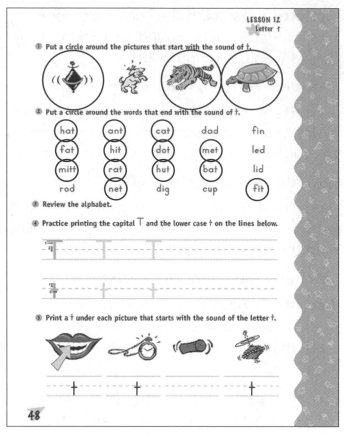

Activity 2. Read the words together. Put a circle around the words that END with the sound of t.

Words:	hat	ant	cat	dad	fin
	fat	hit	dot	met	led
	mitt	rat	hut	bat	lid
	rod	net	dig	cup	fit

Activities 3 & 4. Review the alphabet. Practice printing the capital **T** and lowercase **t** on the lines below. Have the children note that the lowercase **t** crosses the straight line between the top and bottom lines.

Activity 5. Discuss the pictures and their meanings. Print a **t** under each picture that starts with the sound of the letter **t**.

Pictures: **tooth, time, log, top**

Activity 6. Read the sentences together. Print them on the lines below. Remind the student to put a capital letter at the beginning of the sentence and a period at the end.

Sentences: **Tad had a hat.**
Ted had a tug.
Dad had a dog.

Activity 7. Have the student practice printing the letters of the make-up words on the board. Then the student can read the make-up words.

Make-up Words: **tup, teb, taf, tud**

Activity 8. Read each puzzle sentence and draw a line to the picture it matches.

Sentences: **Ben has a dog on a tug.**
Ted has a big dot on a bed.

Activity 9. Practice printing the letter **t** with the vowel letter. Say the sound as you print the letters.

Beginnings: **ta**
te
ti
to
tu

Activity 10. On the white board review the vowel sounds with the **t** preceding them. Student will put a circle around each word that starts like the beginning letters.

ta	tab	sack	tan	tablet
te	test	telephone	ten	bed
ti	film	tip	tin	tick
to	foot	top	toss	tot
tu	tub	tug	tuff	put

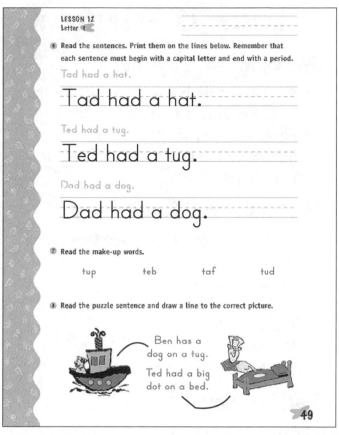

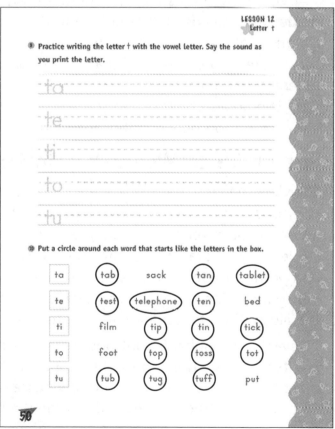

Lesson 13 - Letter n

Overview:

- Review the names and sounds for the alphabet letters studied
- Review the Vowel Rule
- Introduce the letter **n**—its name, sound, and shape

Materials and Supplies:

- Teacher's Guide & Student Workbook
- White board
- Alphabet Story
- Alphabet Poem
- Alphabet flow chart
- Flashcards
- Reader 1: *The Fish Net*

Teaching Tips:

Advise the students that the sound of **n** is made with the lips slightly open and the tongue is at the top of the front teeth. Make sure they understand that the lips are different when making the sound of **m**. Care should also be taken so there is not visual confusion between the **m** and **n**.

Introduction to Workbook Activities:

Review the alphabet story and the alphabet poem. Use the illustrations that go with the letters as flashcards. With daily practice the students will be able to recite the sentences and pronounce the words with the correct initial sounds. The students can color copies of the illustrations for additional reinforcement.

Review the alphabet. Introduce the letter **n**—its name, sound, and shape. Demonstrate on the board the capital **N** and lowercase **n**. Discuss the pictures and have the student recognize and repeat the word so the beginning sound is distinct.

Pictures: **neck, net, nurse, nut, Ned, nail**

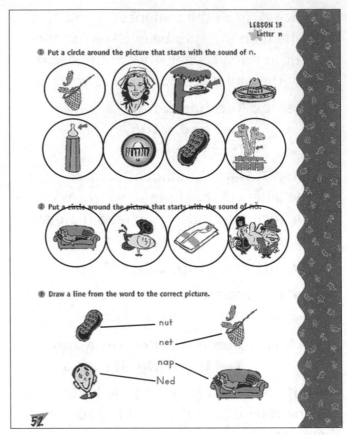

Activity 1. Student will study the pictures and identify the beginning sounds.
Put a circle around the picture that starts with the sound of **n**. Print the letter under each picture that starts with the sound of **n**.

Pictures: **net, nurse, nest, hat nipple, nickle, nut, neck**

Activity 2. Review the vowels with the sound of **n** preceding it. Identify the pictures. Student will put a circle around the pictures that start with the sound of **na**.

Pictures: **nap, Nan, napkin, nab**

Activity 3. Draw a line from the word to the picture it matches.

Pictures: **nut, net, Ned, nap**

Activities 4 & 5. Review the alphabet. Practice printing the capital **N** and lowercase letter **n** on the lines below.

Activity 6. Student will read the words that start with the consonant **n,** then print them on the lines below.

   Words: **Ned, nap, Nan, net**

Activity 7. Spell the words to match the pictures.

   Words: **pan, ran, nut**

Activity 8. Read the words in the word bank together and discuss the meaning of each. Read the sentences together and try the various words for each blank.

  Sentences: Nan had a (**nap**).
                  Ned had his lips on a (**nut**).
                  The (**fan**) is in the den.
                  Dad (**ran**) up a hill.

Activity 9. Practice printing the following words and phrases:

  Words: **fun, fan, nap, pan**
  Phrases: **a bun on a bed**
                 a hat on a hut

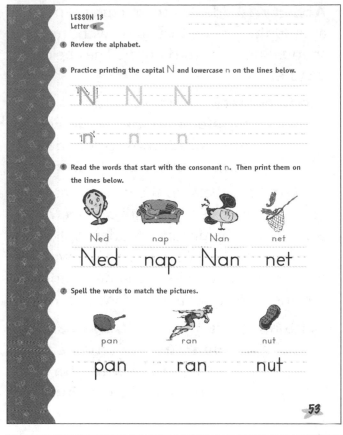

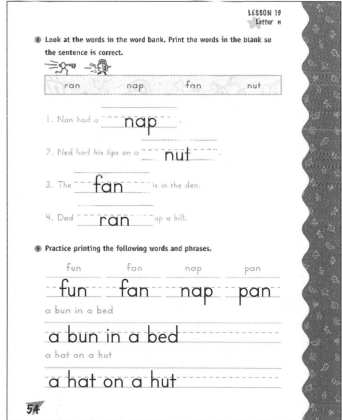

Activity 10. Identify the pictures. Put a circle around the picture that starts with the given sound. Print the word on the lines below the picture.

Pictures: **neck, mess, nest, net**
nipple, men, nickel, newspaper
nut, number, nugget, nap
nod, notch, nostril, number

Activity 11. Work on the white board with a review of words ending with **an**, **en**, **in** and **un**. Identify the pictures. Student will put a circle around the picture that ends with the given sound and write the ending sound on the lines below the appropriate picture.

Pictures:
fan	van	Dan	pan
Ben	hen	men	pen
pin	tin	win	fin
sun	run	fun	bun

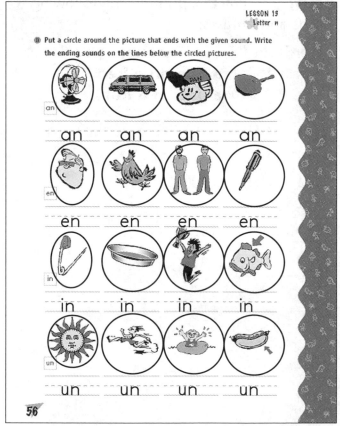

Lesson 14 - Letter k

Overview:

- Review the names and sounds for the alphabet letters already studied
- Introduce the consonant **k**—its name, sound, and shape

Materials and Supplies:

- Teacher's Guide & Student Workbook
- White board
- Alphabet Story
- Alphabet Poem
- Alphabet flow chart
- Flashcards
- Reader 1: *Ken's Kitten*

Teaching Tips:

Encourage the students to print on the board before each printing activity. Stress the formation of the letter **k** in both capital and lowercase letters.

Introduction to Workbook Activities:

Review the alphabet story and the alphabet poem. Use the illustrations that go with the letters as flashcards. With daily practice the students will be able to recite the sentences and pronounce the words with the correct initial sounds. The students can color copies of the illustrations for additional reinforcement.

Review the alphabet. Introduce the letter **k**—the name, sound, and shape. Discuss the pictures and have the students repeat the words until the sound is distinct. Mention that **k** and **c** have the same sound and are often used together at the end of many words.

Pictures: **kite, kick, Ken, Kim, kangaroo, kitten**

Activity 1. Identify the pictures and discuss the meaning for vocabulary enrichment. Student will put a circle around each picture that starts with the sound of **k**.

Pictures: **kangaroo, kettle, kite, tree house, keg, kick, kitten**

Activity 2. Review the vowel sounds with the letter **k** preceding each vowel. Student will circle the words that start like the beginning letters in the box.

Words: **kit   kitten   hid   kid**
       kettle   kite   ketchup Ken

Activity 3. Read the puzzle phrases together. Draw a line from the puzzle phrase to the picture it matches.

Pictures: **a king on a kettle**
            a kid can kick
            ketchup on a kite
            a kitten on a kangaroo

Activities 4 & 5. Review the alphabet. Point out how the capital **K** and lowercase **k** are alike and how they are different. Student will practice printing the capital **K** and lowercase **k** on the lines below.

Activity 6. Look at the pictures. Discuss their meaning. Print **k** under each picture that starts with the sound of **k**.

   Pictures: **kangaroo, kitten, kid, kick**

Activity 7. Read the words and print them on the lines below.

   Words: **kit, tab, Ken**

Activity 8. Read the make-up words.

   Make-up Words: **ket, kag, keb, kif**

Activity 9. Read the following sentences together. Draw a line to the one that matches the picture.

   Pictures: **Ted had the bug.**
   The kangaroo had a king.
   Ed can kick the can.
   Ken had a cat.

Activity 10. Read the sentences. Student will print them on the lines below.

   Ken had fun.
   Dad fed the cub.
   Ed can kick.

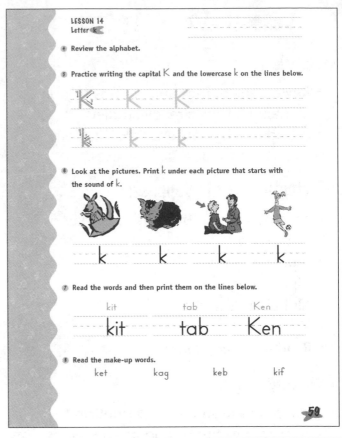

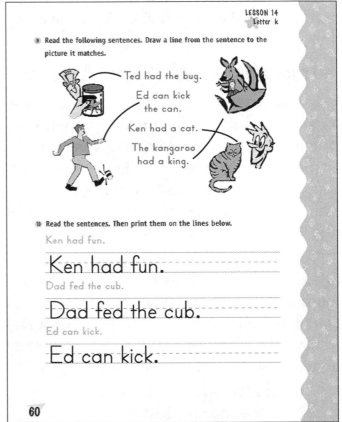

Activity 11. Match the spelling words with the pictures.

    Pictures: **kid, kick, Ken, kitten, kit**

Activity 12. Use the white board to practice completing a spelling word by finishing either a beginning or ending sound. Look at the pictures. Identify the sound that will complete the spelling letter at the beginning of each word. Finish spelling the words that begin with **k**.

    Pictures: **k**iss, **k**ite, **k**ettle, cat

                 kit, dad, **k**ing, **K**im

Activity 13. Read the sentences with the student. Remind them to begin the sentence with a capital letter and end with a period.

  Ed had a bug.
  Dad had a dog.
  Bob fed a dog.
  The big bug dug.

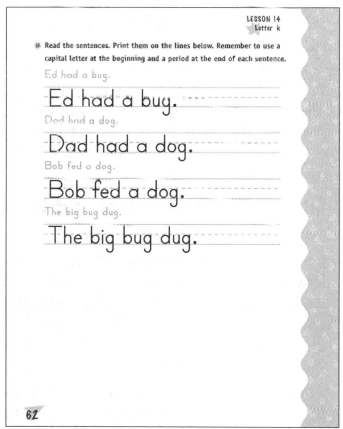

Lesson 15 - Letter l

Overview:

- Review the names and sounds for the alphabet studied
- Review Vowel Rules
- Introduce the letter **l**—its name, sound, and shape through pictures

Materials and Supplies:

- Teacher's Guide & Student Workbook
- White board
- Alphabet Story
- Alphabet Poem
- Alphabet flow chart
- Flashcards
- Reader 1: *Les Can Lift*

Teaching Tips:

Use flashcards as a tool for review. Spread out those that have been studied. Have the student select certain vowels as you direct. Then have them pick out a consonant for the beginning of a word. The activity can be reversed by having the student use an ending letter. Complete a word by adding one more letter. Let the student decide if it is a real or make-up word.

Introduction to Workbook Activities:

Review the alphabet story and the alphabet poem. Use the illustrations that go with the letters as flashcards. With daily practice the students will be able to recite the sentences and pronounce the words with the correct initial sounds. The students can color copies of the illustrations for additional reinforcement.

Review the alphabet. Introduce the letter **l**—the name, sound, and shape. Have the student recognize the pictures and repeat the word so the beginning sound is distinct.

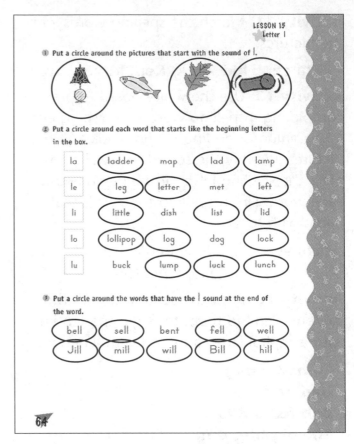

Study the pictures used to identify the consonant sound of **l**.

Pictures: **lion, lock, lamp, lunch, lily**

Activity 1. Identify the pictures so the sound of **l** is distinct. Student will put a circle around the pictures that start with the sound of **l**.

Pictures: **lamp, fish, leaf, log**

Activity 2. On the white board, have the student practice printing the letter **l** with the all the vowels. In the workbook, the student will put a circle around each word that starts like the given beginning letters.

Words:			
ladder	**map**	**lad**	**lamp**
leg	**letter**	**met**	**left**
little	**dish**	**list**	**lid**
lollipop	**log**	**dog**	**lock**
buck	**lump**	**luck**	**lunch**

Activity 3. Discuss the use of the letter **l** at the end of a word. The double **l** at the end of the word does not change the sound. Student will circle the words that have the sound of **l** at the end of the word.

Words: **bell   sell   bent   fell   well**
       Jill   mill   will   Bill   hill

Activities 4 & 5. Review the alphabet. Discuss the beginning and the formation of the letter **l**. Have the students follow the numbers for directional clues. Print the capital **L** and lowercase letter **l**.

Activity 6. Identify the pictures. Print the letter **l** under each picture that starts with the sound of letter **l**.

Pictures: **lamp, ladder, legs, lizard**

Activity 7. Student will look at the words that start with the letter **l** and then print them on the lines below.

Words: **lamb, lock, little, log**

Activity 8. Read the words in the word bank together and discuss the meaning of each. Read the sentences together and try the various words for each blank. Make them aware that there is an extra word offered. Student will print the words in the blanks to make a complete sentence.

Sentences: Ken had a (**lock**) in his hand.
          The (**lad**) can kick.
          Ed is a (**little**) boy.

Activity 9. Have the student read the words. Practice printing them on the white board before printing in the workbook.

Words: **log   lot   lad   left**
       leg   lid   lug   lob

Activity 10. Read the make-up words.

Make-up Words: **lub, lom, lig, lat, len, lof**

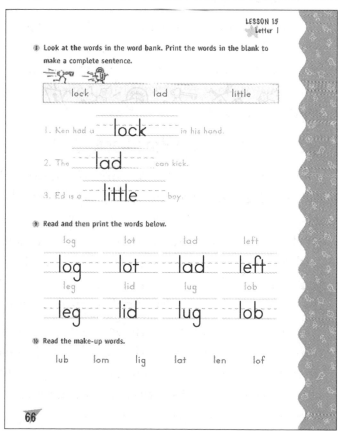

Lesson 16 - Letter m

Overview:

- Review the name and sound for the consonants and vowels that have been studied
- Review the vowels and the Vowel Rules.
- Introduce the letter **m**—its name, sound, and shape through pictures

Materials and Supplies:

- Teacher's Guide & Student Workbook
- White board
- Alphabet Story
- Alphabet Poem
- Alphabet flow chart
- Flashcards
- Reader 1: *The Mask*

Teaching Tips:

Care must be taken to assure the student sees and hears the difference between the consonant sounds **m** and **n**. From dictation, have the student use the white board to print the letter **m** with all the vowels.

Introduction to Workbook Activities:

Review the alphabet story and the alphabet poem. Use the illustrations that go with the letters as flashcards. With daily practice the students will be able to recite the sentences and pronounce the words with the correct initial sounds. The students can color copies of the illustrations for additional reinforcement.

Review the alphabet. Introduce the consonant **m**—its name, sound, and shape. Do all of these activities together. Have the student recognize the pictures and repeat the word so the beginning sound is distinct.

Pictures: **mask, mouse, mug, monkey, muffin**

Activities 1 & 2. Review the alphabet. Begin printing capital **M** and lowercase **m**. Use the board for demonstration of all printing. Have the student note beginning and each additional stroke.

Activity 3. Read the words that start with the consonant **m**. Print them on the lines below.

Words: **milk, mat, man**

Activity 4. Read the words in the word bank together and discuss the meaning of each. Have the student try each of the words in the different blanks and decide if the meaning is correct. Print the word in the blank to complete the sentence.

Sentences: The (**mill**) is on the hill.
Dad had a (**mug**) in his hand.
The dog sat on a (**mat**).

Activity 5. The student will spell the words to match each picture.

    Pictures: **mat, mug, mill**
               mad, mess, milk

Activity 6. Read the funny sentences together. Draw a line from the picture to the sentence it matches.

    Sentences: **The man had a mug.**
               Meg had mud in the milk.
               Ted had a mat on the leg.

Activity 7. Study the pictures so the student can identify words starting with the letter **m**. Make the student aware of the difference between the **m** and **n** printed formation. Put a circle around the picture that starts with the sound of **m**. Write the letters under each picture that starts with **m**.

    Pictures: **ant, mitten, monkey, mom**

Activity 8. Have the students make up their own words by using the flashcards. Keep it in game form for fun. This is a determining factor to see if the student needs more drill.

    Make-up Words: **maf, meb, mip, mot, mun**

Activity 9. Review the consonant **m** sound with all of the vowels. Have the student read each set of pictures and discuss the words. Have the student look at the beginning sounds of the given letter. Print the specified beginning letters under each picture.

    Pictures:

map	**mad**	**ostrich**	**mask**
mess	**pan**	**medicine**	**melon**

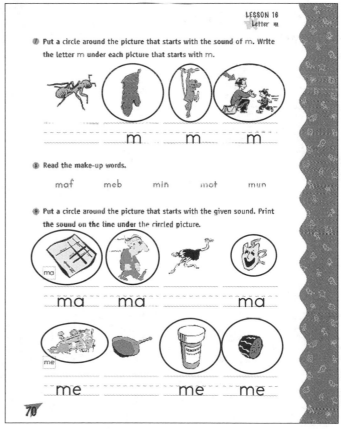

Activity 10. Have the student read each set of pictures and discuss the words. Have the student look at the beginning sounds of the given letters. Print the specified beginning letters under each picture.

Pictures:

men	**mixer**	**mitt**	**milk**
moth	**mop**	**mom**	**bat**
mug	**muffin**	**mushroom**	**lock**

Activity 11. Practice printing the following words and funny phrases.

Words: **man, ham, men, Meg**
Phrases: **a man on a mat**
        a hat on a cat

Activity 12. Read the funny sentences together. Draw a line from the picture to the sentence it matches.

A cat had a log.
The bed is on a doll.
Ed had a big hog.
Dad had a leg on a dog.

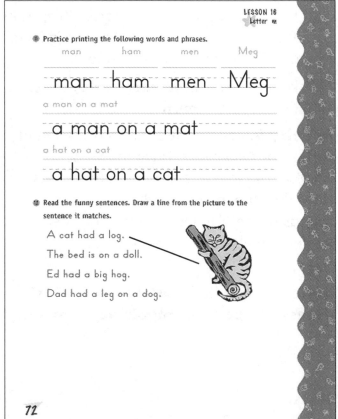

Lesson 17 - Letter p

Overview:

- Review the names and sounds for the letters studied
- Review Vowel Rule
- Introduce the letter **p**—its name, sound, and shape
- The letter **p** will be used at either the beginning or ending of a word
- Review the letter **s** used as a plural

Materials and Supplies:

- Teacher's Guide & Student Workbook
- White board
- Alphabet Story
- Alphabet Poem
- Alphabet flow chart
- Flashcards
- Reader 1: *The Puppy*

Teaching Tips:

- Distinguish the placement of the breath when making the sounds of the letters **p** and **b**.
- Review all five vowels with the beginning consonant **p**.
- Identify the letter **p** at the beginning and ending of a word.

Introduction to Workbook Activities:

Review the alphabet story and the alphabet poem. Use the illustrations that go with the letters as flashcards. With daily practice the students will be able to recite the sentences and pronounce the words with the correct initial sounds. The students can color copies of the illustrations for additional reinforcement.

Review the alphabet. Introduce the letter **p**—the name, sound, and shape. Have the student recognize the pictures and repeat the word so the beginning is distinct.

Pictures: **parrot, pig, pin, paint, pan**

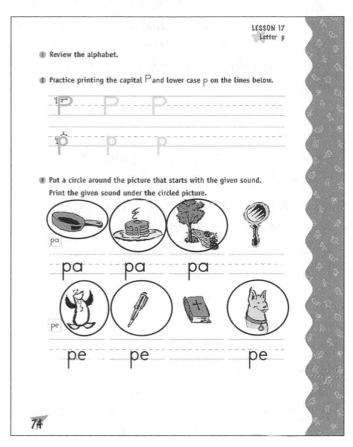

Activities 1 & 2. Review the alphabet. Discuss the beginning and the formation of the letter **p**. Note should be made that the lowercase **p** goes below the bottom line. Have the students follow the numbers for directional clues. Print the capital **P** and lowercase **p**.

Activity 3. On the white board, have the student practice printing the letter **p** with all the vowels. In the workbook, the student will put a circle around each word that starts with the given beginning letters and the print the letters.

Words:

pan	**pancakes**	**path**	**mirror**
penguin	**pen**	**Bible**	**pet**

Activity 4. In the workbook, the student will put a circle around each word that starts with the given beginning letters and then print the letters.

Words:

monkey	**pin**	**pillow**	**picnic**
popcorn	**mop**	**pocket**	**pot**
puddle	**pumpkin**	**puppy**	**jug**

Activity 5. The sight word **is** must be taught ahead of time. Have the student print **is** on the board. Read the funny sentences. Draw a line from the picture to the sentence it matches.

A pad is in the mud.
A pup is in a pan.
A pin is on a pig.

Activity 6. Discuss the letter **s** used as a plural. Students should be aware of the sound of **p** at the end of the word as well as at the beginning. Read the words. Draw a line from the word to the correct picture.

Pictures: **pup, pans, pins, pens**

Activity 7. Read the words. Draw a line from the word to the correct picture.

Pictures: **map, pump, top, cap**

Activity 8. Read the words that start with the consonant **p**. Print the words on the lines below.

Words: **pig, pet, pin, pen**

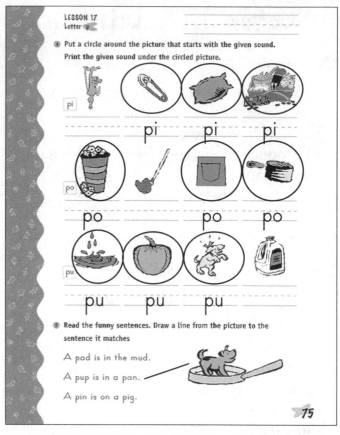

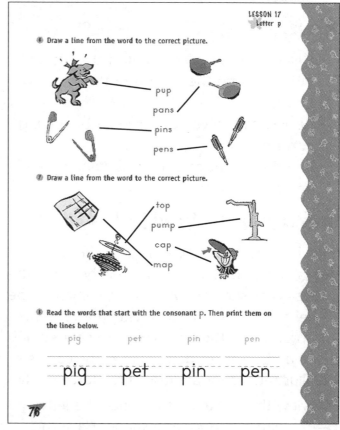

Activity 9. Identify the pictures so the sound of **p** is distinct. Put a circle around the pictures that start with the sound of **p**. Print the letter **p** under each picture that starts with that sound.

   Pictures: **paint, bell, purse, pie**

Activity 10. Read the make-up words.

   Make-up Words: **pud, pom, pib, paf, ped**

Activity 11. Dictate the words slowly so that the student can spell the words to match the pictures.

   Words: **pad, peg, pan pit, pet, pop**

Activity 12. Practice printing the following words and phrases.

   Words: **pill, pod, map, lap**
   Phrases: **a pig and a fan a pig in a pan**

Activity 13. Read the words in the word bank together and discuss the meaning of each. Read the sentences and try the various words for each blank. Student will print the words in the blanks to make a complete sentence.

   The man had a (**pig**) in the barn.
   Mom has a (**pan**) in her hand.
   Peg can (**mend**) the pants.

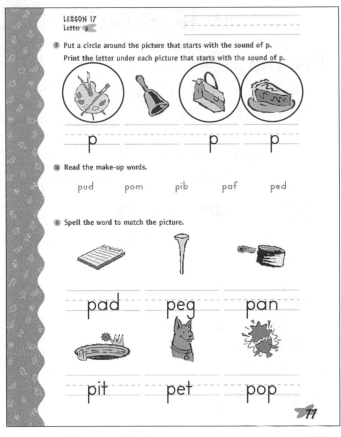

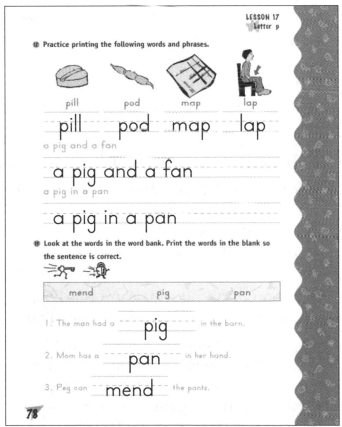

Lesson 18 - Letter r

Overview:

- Review the names and sounds for the alphabet studied
- Review the Vowel Rules
- Introduce the letter **r**
- Develop an awareness of spelling

Materials and Supplies:

- Teacher's Guide & Student Workbook
- White board
- Alphabet Story
- Alphabet Poem
- Alphabet flow chart
- Flashcards
- Reader 1: *The Rag Doll*

Teaching Tips:

Introduce the consonant **r**—its name, sound, and shape. Use flashcards as a tool for review. Have the student match the flashcards to the letters on the alphabet flow chart. Review the vowel sounds. Show the student the importance of putting letters together for a spelling list.

Introduction to Workbook Activities:

Review the alphabet story and the alphabet poem. Use the illustrations that go with the letters as flashcards. With daily practice the students will be able to recite the sentences and pronounce the words with the correct initial sounds. The students can color copies of the illustrations for additional reinforcement.

Review the alphabet. Introduce the letter **r**—its name, sound, and shape. Have the student recognize the pictures and repeat the word so the beginning sound is distinct. Study the pictures used to identify the consonant sound of **r**.

Pictures: **raccoon, rocket, rake, rabbit, rooster, rat**

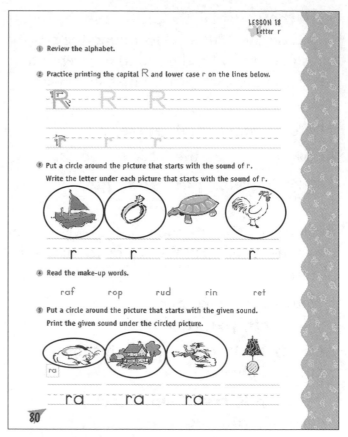

Activities 1 & 2. Review the alphabet. Discuss the beginning and the formation of the letter **r**. Have the students follow the numbers for directional clues.

Print the capital **R** and lowercase letter **r**.

Activity 3. Identify the pictures so the sound of **r** is distinct. Student will circle the picture that starts with the sound of **r**. Print the letter under each word that begins with the sound of **r**.

Pictures: **raft, ring, turtle, rooster**

Activity 4. Have the student read the make-up words. Practice printing them on the white board before printing in the workbook.

Make-up Words: **raf, rop, rud, rin, ret**

Activity 5. On the white board, have the student practice printing the letter **r** with all of the vowels. In the workbook, the student will put a circle around each word that starts like the given beginning letter. Print the given sound under the circled picture.

Words: **rabbit, ranch, ran, lamp**

Activity 6. The students will put a circle around the picture that starts with the given sound, then print the given sound under the circled picture.

Words: **leaf, rent, red, rest**
rink, ring, pin, ribbon
puppy, rock, rocket, rod
mug, rug, rubber band, run

Activity 7. Read the words. Draw a line from the word to the picture it matches.

Pictures: **rip, run, red, rat, rod**

Activity 8. Read the words in the word bank together and discuss the meaning of each. Read the sentences together and try the various words for each blank. Print the words in the blanks to complete each sentence.

The big (**rat**) had a hat.
Ed sat on a (**raft**).
Rod can (**run**) in the sun.

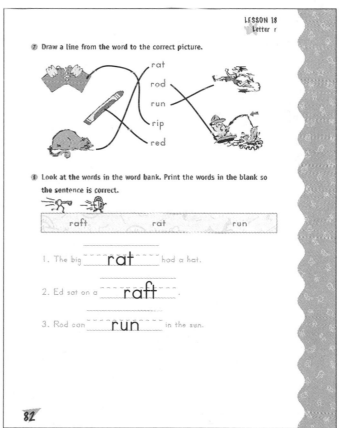

Activity 9. Read the funny sentences together. Draw a line from the picture to the sentence it matches.

Sentences: **A rip is in a pan.**
A rug is on a rocker.
A rag is on a rat.

Activity 10. Read the words together. Practice printing the words beginning with **r**.

Words: **rabbit, rest, rat, rub**

Activity 11. Student will identify the pictures that start with the consonant **r**.
Have them print the words below the picture.

Pictures: **rod, run, red, rip**

Activity 12. Practice printing the words beginning with **r**.

Words: **ranch, ram, ribbon**

Activity 13. Read the words together. Draw a line from the word to the picture it matches.

Pictures: **rap, raft, rod, rip, run, red**

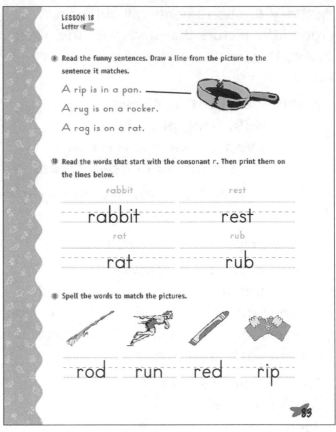

Lesson 19 - Letter s

Overview:

- Review the names and sounds for the alphabet studied
- Review the Vowel Rules
- Introduce the letter **s**
- Capital letters for names

Materials and Supplies:

- Teacher's Guide & Student Workbook
- White board
- Alphabet Story
- Alphabet Poem
- Alphabet flow chart
- Flashcards
- Reader 1: *The Socks*

Teaching Tips:

In teaching the printing of the letter **s**, make sure that the student starts at the upper right side of the letter to avoid reversals. Make note that the word **sis** is not capitalized unless it is used as a name. Use flashcards to review the letters. Include each of the vowels following the letter **s** for drill and practice.

Introduction to Workbook Activities:

Review the alphabet story and the alphabet poem. Use the illustrations that go with the letters as flashcards. With daily practice the students will be able to recite the sentences and pronounce the words with the correct initial sounds. The students can color copies of the illustrations for additional reinforcement.

Review the alphabet. Introduce the letter **s**— its name, sound, and shape. Have the student recognize the pictures and repeat the word so the beginning sound is distinct. Study the pictures used to identify the consonant sound of **s**.

Pictures: **seal, sat, socks, sand, sail**

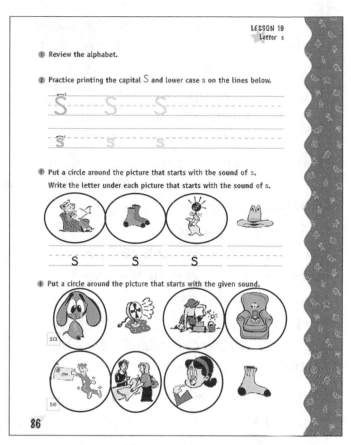

Activities 1 & 2. Review the alphabet. Discuss the beginning and the formation of the letter **s**. Have the students follow the numbers for directional clues.

Print the capital **S** and lowercase letter **s**.

Activity 3. Identify the pictures so the sound of **s** is distinct. Student will print the letter under the picture that starts with the sound of **s**.

Pictures: **sit, socks, seal, hat**

Activity 4. On the white board, have the student practice printing the letter **s** with all of the vowels. In the workbook, the student will put a circle around the pictures that start with the given sound.

Pictures: **sad, fan, sand, sat send, sell, self, sock**

Activity 5. In the workbook, the student will put a circle around the pictures that start with the given sound.

   Pictures: **sick, lip, sip, sift**
   　　　　　Tom, sob, sock, song
   　　　　　suds, gum, sun, sum

Activity 6. Read the sentences together. Draw a line to the picture that tells about the sentence.

   Sam sat in a tub.
   Ned and Nell can sell the pans.
   The big red fan is in the mud.
   Bill hid in the pen.

Activity 7. Have the student read the words that start with the consonant **s**, then print them on the lines below.

   Words: **Sam, sad, sun, sill**

Activity 8. Have the student practice spelling the words on the white board. Then spell the words in the workbook to match the pictures.

   Words: **sat, sip, sun**

Activity 9. Use white board to demonstrate the letter **s** coming at the end of a word. Identify the pictures and have the students underline the pictures that END with the sound of **s**.

   Words: **gas, mess, pill, Bess**

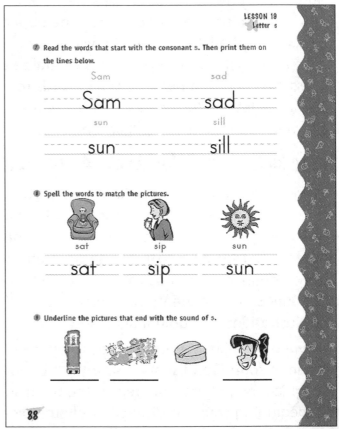

Horizons Kindergarten Phonics and Reading

Activity 10. Look at the words in the word bank together and discuss the meaning of each. Read the sentences together and try the various words for each blank. Print the word in the blank so the sentence is correct.

Sentences: Meg can (**sit**) in the sun.
Sip the (**soup**) in a mug.
Ed can (**toss**) a rock.
Jan sat on the (**sill**).
The boy played in the (**sand**).
Tom will (**sing**) a song.

Activity 11. Practice printing the following words and phrases.

Words: **mess, miss, send, sand**
Phrases: **sit in the sun**
sit on a big hill
sit on a rug
sit on a sill

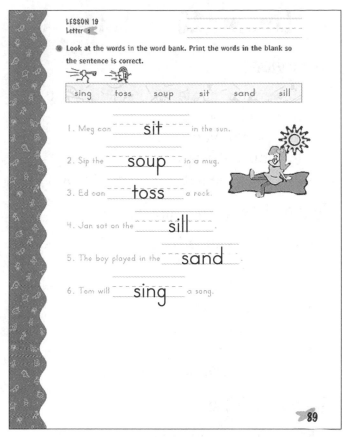

Lesson 20 - Letter q

Overview:

- Review the names and sounds for the alphabet studied
- Review the Vowel Rule
- Introduce the letter **q**
- Rule that the letter **u** always follows the **q**

Materials and Supplies:

- Teacher's Guide & Student Workbook
- White board
- Alphabet Story
- Alphabet Poem
- Alphabet flow chart
- Flashcards
- Reader 1: *Quacker, the Duck*

Teaching Tips:

Review the names and sounds for the alphabet studied. Reinforce the need for having a vowel in a word. Explain that the **q** has the sound of "**cue**." Explain that **qu** together makes a sound like **kw** blended.

Introduction to Workbook Activities:

Review the alphabet story and the alphabet poem. Use the illustrations that go with the letters as flashcards. With daily practice the students will be able to recite the sentences and pronounce the words with the correct initial sounds. The students can color copies of the illustrations for additional reinforcement.

Review the alphabet. Introduce the letter **q**—the name, sound, and shape. Discuss the need for always having the letter **u** following the **q**. At the beginning of a word, it makes the sound of **kw** blended. Have the student study the pictures and repeat the word so the beginning sound of **qu** is distinct.

Pictures: **quilt, queen, quiver, quail, quarter**

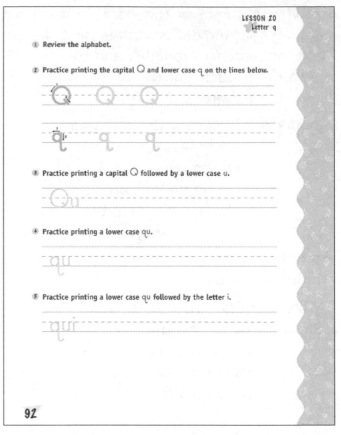

Activities 1 & 2. Review the alphabet. Have the student notice that the lowercase **q** has a tail that comes below the bottom line. The tail of the **q** curves to the right (to make a place for the **u** to follow). Care should be taken that the student does not mix the printing of a lowercase **g** where the tail below the line curves to the left. Be sure to have the student note that the circle part of the **q** is made first, then the curved tail. Often there is a reversal of **p** and **q**. Practice printing the capital **Q** and the lowercase **q**.

Activity 3. Practice printing a capital **Q** followed by a lowercase **u**.

Activity 4. Practice printing a lowercase **qu**.

Activity 5. Practice printing a lowercase **qu** followed by the letter **i**.

Activity 6. Identify the pictures so the sound of **qu** is distinct. Put a circle around the pictures that start with the sound of **qu**. Print the letters **qu** under each picture starting with that sound.

Pictures: **quarter, quail, piano, queen**

Activity 7. Underline the **qu** in each word that begins with the sound of **qu**.

Words: **quilt, quiver, quit, quiet, quiz**

Activity 8. Read the words together. Draw a line from the picture to the correct word.

Pictures: **quail, quilt, quiet, queen, quill**

Activity 9. Read the following sentences together. Emphasize that each sentence must have a capital letter for the first word and a period at the end of the sentence. Print the sentences on the lines below the picture. Review the plural **s** as used in the word **quail**. Discuss how the baby birds follow their parents.

The queen is quiet.
The mom and dad quail had little quails.
The little tot sat on a quilt.
Nan had to quit the run.

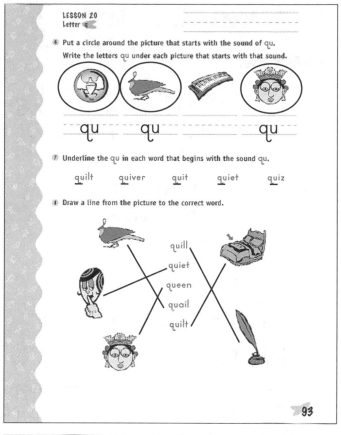

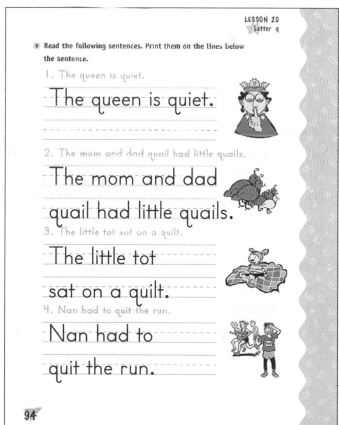

Lesson 21 - Letter j

Overview:

- Review the names and sounds for the alphabet letters that have been studied
- Introduce the consonant **j**—its name, sound, and shape

Materials and Supplies:

- Teacher's Guide & Student Workbook
- Alphabet Story
- Alphabet Poem
- Alphabet flow chart
- Flashcards
- Reader 1: *The Jack-in-the-Box*

Teaching Tips:

No word in the American language ends with the letter **j**. The sound of **j** heard in the word "**judge**" will be taught later.

Introduction to Workbook Activities:

Review the alphabet story and the alphabet poem. Use the illustrations that go with the letters as flashcards. With daily practice the students will be able to recite the sentences and pronounce the words with the correct initial sounds. The students can color copies of the illustrations for additional reinforcement.

Review the alphabet. Introduce the letter **j**— its name, sound, and shape. Have the student recognize the pictures and repeat the word so the beginning sound is distinct. Study the pictures used to identify the consonant sound of **j**.

Pictures: **jam, juice, jet, jack-in-the-box, jacket**

Activities 1 & 2. Review the alphabet. Discuss the beginning and the formation of the letter **j**. Have the students follow the directional clues. Practice printing the capital **J** and the lowercase **j**. Be sure to indicate that the lowercase **j** goes below the bottom line and has a dot above it.

Activity 3. Identify the pictures so the sound of **j** is distinct. Student will put a circle around the pictures that start with the sound of **j**. Print the letter **j** under each picture with that sound.

Words: **jug, jar, jack-in-the-box, jump**

Activity 4. Read the words that start with the consonant **j** and print them on the lines below.

Words: **Jill, jig, job**

Horizons Kindergarten Phonics and Reading

Activity 5. Draw a line from the picture to the word it matches.

Pictures: **jacket, jack-in-the-box, jump, jelly, job**

Activity 6. Read the words in the word bank together and discuss the meaning of each. Read the sentences together and try the various words for each blank.

Sentences: (**Jack**) can run a lot.
Can Jon (**jog**) to the pond?
Did Meg get a (**job**)?

Activity 7. Read the sentences together. Draw a line to the picture that tells about the sentence.

Pictures: **Jill sat on a cot.
Jack can jig.
The jug is in the mud.
Jim had a big job.**

Activity 8. On the white board, have the student practice printing the letter **j** with all the vowels. Make use of the flashcards in conjunction with a game activity of having the student print letters. Identify all the pictures so the beginning consonant/vowel sounds are distinct. Put a circle around the picture that starts with the given sound. Print the given sound under the circled picture.

Words:

**gift   jacket   jacks   jam
Jen   jet   Jed   jelly**

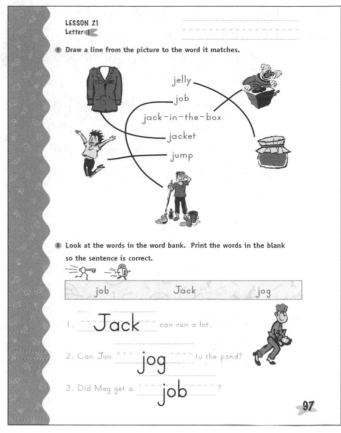

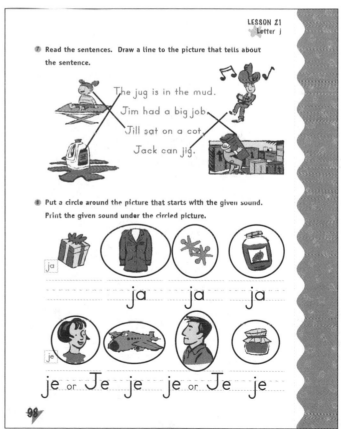

Activity 9. Have the student circle the picture that starts with the given sound.
Print the given sound under the circled picture.

Words:

Jill	**Jim**	**Bill**	**jig**
jog	**dot**	**jot**	**Jon**
gull	**jug**	**jump**	**junk**

Activity 10. Spell the words to match the pictures.

Pictures: **jog, junk, jet**
jug, jam, jump

Activity 11. Practice printing the following words and phrases.

Words: **jet, job, Jack**
Phrases: **a jug in the mud**
a bell on a jet

Lesson 22 - Letter v

Overview:

- Review the names and sounds for the alphabet studied
- Review the Vowel Rule
- Introduce the letter **v**—its name, sound, and shape

Materials and Supplies:

- Teacher's Guide & Student Workbook
- White board
- Alphabet Story
- Alphabet Poem
- Alphabet flow chart
- Flashcards
- Reader 1: *The Vests*

Teaching Tips:

Encourage the student to read words and sentences silently at first. Try to make it a puzzle or game to figure out the answers. Keep an enthusiastic attitude at all times.

Introduction to Workbook Activities:

Review the alphabet story and the alphabet poem. Use the illustrations that go with the letters as flashcards. With daily practice the students will be able to recite the sentences and pronounce the words with the correct initial sounds. The students can color copies of the illustrations for additional reinforcement.

Review the alphabet. Introduce the letter **v**—its name, sound, and shape. Point out that the **v** has a sharp point at the bottom in contrast to the curved **u**. Have the students recognize the pictures and repeat the word so the beginning sound is distinct. Study the pictures used to identify the consonant sound of **v**.

Pictures: **vest, veil, volcano, vacuum, vet, van**

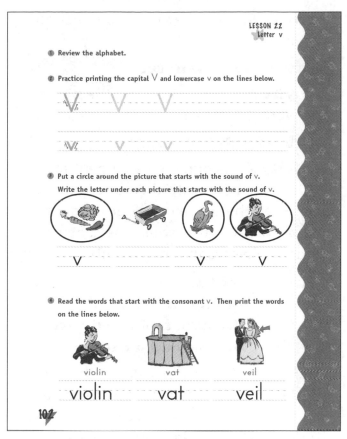

Activities 1 & 2. Review the alphabet. Discuss the formation of the letter **v**—its beginning and sharp point at the bottom. Practice printing the capital **V** and lowercase **v** on the lines below.

Activity 3. Identify the pictures so the sound of **v** is distinct. Monitor it closely so there is not the sound of **b** in its place. Student will put a circle around the pictures that start with the sound of **v**. Print the letter under each picture with that sound.

Pictures: **vegetables, wagon, vulture, violin**

Activity 4. Discuss the words and the pictures. Indicate that some of the vowels cannot use the short vowel sound. Have the student read the words under the pictures. Then print the entire word on the lines below.

Activity 5. Spell the words to match the pictures.

   Pictures: **vest, van, vet**

Activity 6. Draw a line from the picture to the word it matches.

   Pictures: **tub, vet, van, vest**

Activity 7. Encourage the student to read each sentence silently, then discuss it with you. Read the sentences aloud. Draw a line to the picture that tells about the sentence. Underline words that begin with the letter **v**.

   Pictures: **Jim has a vine.**
   Dad has a tan van.
   The man had a red vest.
   The vet had a cat.

Activity 8. On the board have the student practice printing the letter **v** with the **a**, **e**, **i**, **o**, and **u** vowel sounds. In the workbook, the student will put a circle around each word that starts like the given beginning letters. Print the word on the lines below the picture.

   Pictures: **van, sat, vat**
   vest, jet, vet
   visor, vinegar, village
   volume, volcano, vulture

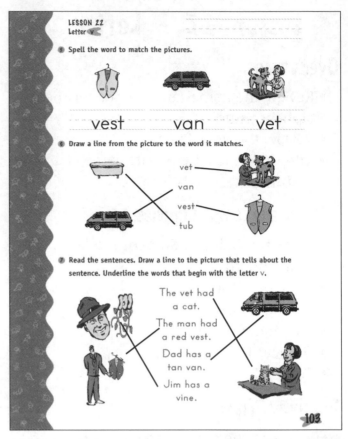

Activity 9. Read the words in the word bank together and discuss the meaning of each. Read the sentences together and try the various words for each blank.

Sentences: The (**vet**) had a pet.
Meg has a (**violin**) lesson.
Jon has a red (**vest**).

Activity 10. Practice printing the following phrases.

Phrases: **a vet can pet**
a van in the sand
the best vest

Activity 11. Practice printing the following words.

Words: **quit   hip   quilt**
quill   quest   pill
pat   quiet   quack

Activity 12. Spell the words to match the pictures.

Pictures: **quick, quilt, cap**
quill, quack, pup

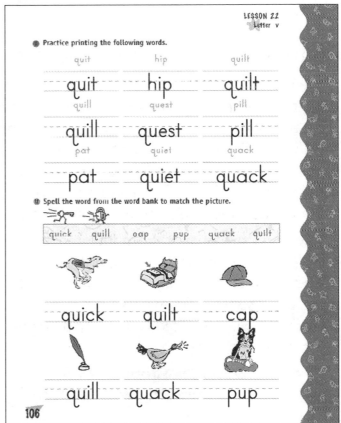

Lesson 23 - Letter w

Overview:

- Review the names and sounds for the alphabet studied
- Review the Vowel Rules
- Introduce the letter **w**

Materials and Supplies:

- Teacher's Guide & Student Workbook
- White board
- Alphabet Story
- Alphabet Poem
- Alphabet flow chart
- Flashcards
- Reader 1: *The Big Wig*

Teaching Tips:

- Introduce the consonant **w**—its name, sound, and shape
- Use flashcards as a tool for review.

Introduction to Workbook Activities:

Review the alphabet story and the alphabet poem. Use the illustrations that go with the letters as flashcards. With daily practice the students will be able to recite the sentences and pronounce the words with the correct initial sounds. The students can color copies of the illustrations for additional reinforcement.

Review the alphabet. Introduce the letter **w**—its name, sound, and shape. Have the students recognize the pictures and repeat the word so the beginning sound is distinct. Study the pictures used to identify the consonant sound of **w**.

Pictures: **watch, wagon, wigwam, web, waffle, watermelon**

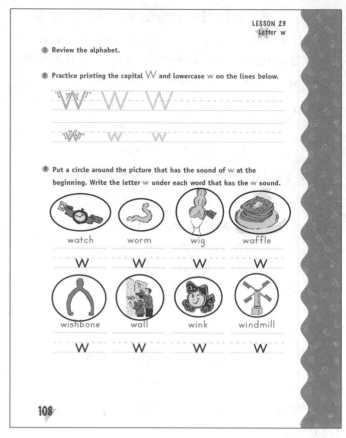

Activities 1 & 2. Review the alphabet, then discuss the beginning and the formation of the letter **w**. Have the students follow the numbers for directional clues. Print the capital **W** and lowercase letter **w**.

Activity 3. Discuss and identify the pictures so the sound of **w** is distinct. Student will circle the pictures that start with the sound of **w**. Print the letter under each word that has the **w** sound.

Pictures: **watch, worm, wig, waffle wishbone, wall, wink, windmill**

Activity 4. Use the white board to have the student printing the make-up words for practice. Have the student read the words.

Make-up Words: **wib, wem, wum, wid**

Activity 5. Read the sentences below. Draw a line from the picture to the sentence it matches.

Pictures: **Jan has a red wig.**
The window is up.
Jim sat in a wigwam.
Mom fed us a watermelon.

Activity 6. Read the funny question sentences together. Discuss the possibility and the probable answer then draw a line from the picture to the sentence it matches.

Sentences: **Is the walrus in the water?**
Is a worm big and fat?
Can a windmill jog?
Did Jon win a waffle?

Activity 7. Read the words together. Have the student draw a line from the picture to the word it matches.

Pictures: **watermelon, window,**
wishbone, web, walrus

Activity 8. Read the words together that start with the consonant **w**, then print the words on the lines below.

Words: **woman, wag, well, web**

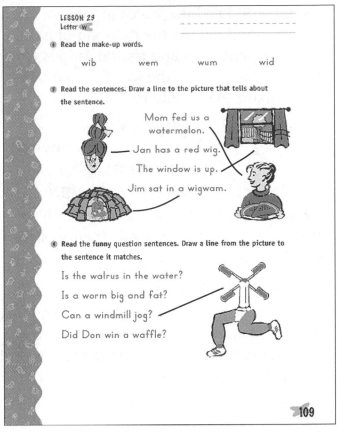

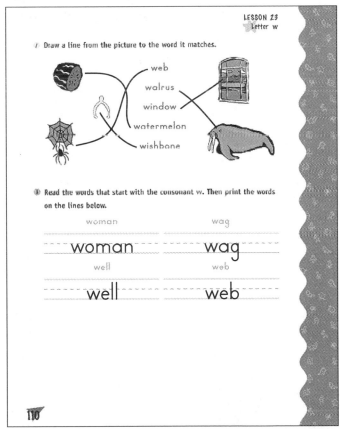

Activity 9. Read the words in the word bank together and discuss the meaning of each. Read the sentences and try the various words for each blank. Print the words in the blanks to complete each sentence.

    Sentences: The (**wigwam**) is on a hill.
                 Dad had a red (**watermelon**).
                 The (**walrus**) sat in the sand.
                 Will you get a red (**wig**)?

Activity 10. Use the white board to have the spelling words practiced. Then spell the words in the workbook.

    Words: **web, wet, wig**

Activity 11. Have the student read and then print the following sentences. Be sure to use a capital letter on the first word and a period or question mark at the end.

    Sentences: **The pup can wag.**
                Jill has a wig.
                Can you jog with Will and Sam?
                Is it red wax?

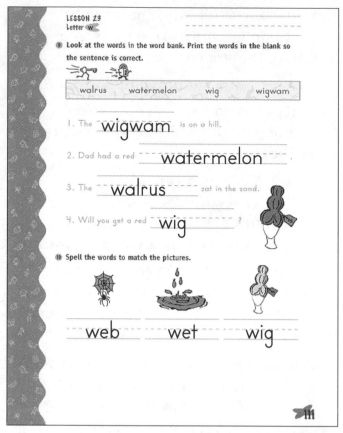

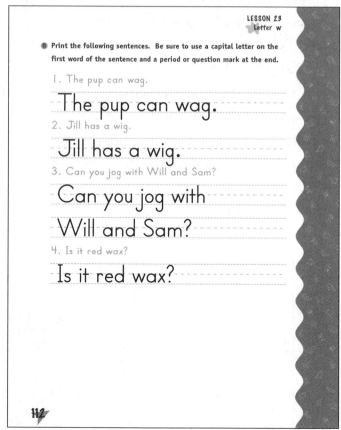

Lesson 24 - Letter y

Overview:

- Review the names and sounds for the alphabet studied
- Review the Vowel Rules
- Introduce the letter **y**—its name, sound, and shape
- Review of question sentences

Materials and Supplies:

- Teacher's Guide & Student Workbook
- White board
- Alphabet Story
- Alphabet Poem
- Alphabet flow chart
- Flashcards
- Reader 1: *The Yo-Yo*

Teaching Tips:

Introduce the consonant **y**. Explain that **y** can also used as a vowel. Example: In the word **by** the letter **y** replaces the regular vowel **i** with the long sound. This will be discussed in more detail in a later lesson.

Introduction to Workbook Activities:

Review the alphabet story and the alphabet poem. Use the illustrations that go with the letters as flashcards. With daily practice the students will be able to recite the sentences and pronounce the words with the correct initial sounds. The students can color copies of the illustrations for additional reinforcement.

Review the alphabet. Introduce the letter **y**— its name, sound, and shape. Have the student recognize the pictures and repeat the word so the beginning sound is distinct. Study the pictures used to identify the sound of the **y** as it is used as a consonant.

Pictures: **yellow, yawn, year, yell, yo-yo, yak**

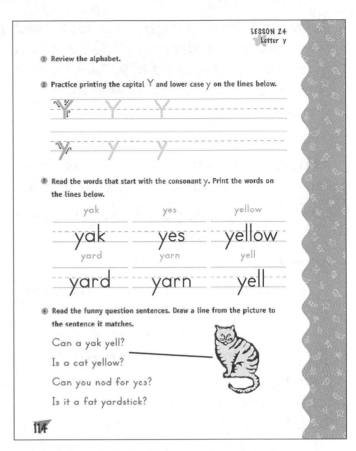

Activities 1 & 2. Review the alphabet. Practice printing the capital **Y** and lowercase **y** on the lines below. Have the students take note that the tail of the lowercase **y** extends below the line.

Activity 3. Read the words that start with the consonant **y**. Print the words on the lines below.

Words: **yak, yes, yellow
yard, yarn, yell**

Activity 4. Read the funny question sentences. Discuss the meaning of the sentence and the possibility of the answer.

Sentences: **Can a yak yell?
Is a cat yellow?
Can you nod for yes?
Is it a fat yardstick?**

Activity 5. Identify the pictures so the sound of **y** is distinct. Student will circle the pictures that start with the sound of **y**. Print the letter under each picture that begins with the sound of **y**.

   Pictures: **yard, yo-yo, yarn, yell**

Activity 6. Read the words together. Draw a line from the picture to the word it matches.

   Pictures: **yams, yardstick, yarn, year, yellow**

Activity 7. Read the sentences.

   Sentences: **Mom has yarn to fix a cap.**
   A yak is in the pen.
   Jan fed us yams.
   Jon has a yellow yo-yo.

Activity 8. Read the words in the word bank together and discuss the meaning of each. Read the sentences together and try the various words for each blank. Print the words in the blanks to complete each sentence.

   Sentences: Can you buy a (**yellow**) yo-yo?
   Dan had a cap of (**yarn**).
   The (**yak**) is very big.
   Jim can nod (**yes**). Can you?

Activity 9. Spell the words to match the pictures.

   Pictures: **up, yak, vet, yell**

Activity 10. Use the white board to have the student practice printing the make-up words. Read the words.

   Make-up Words: **yad, yub, yef, yog**

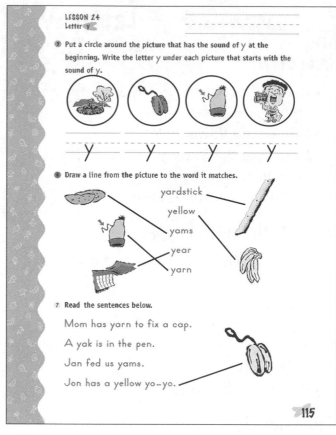

Lesson 25 - Letter z

Overview:

- Review the names and sounds for the alphabet studied
- Review vowels and Vowel Rule
- Introduce the letter **z**—its name, sound, and shape

Materials and Supplies:

- Teacher's Guide & Student Workbook
- White board
- Alphabet Story
- Alphabet Poem
- Alphabet flow chart
- Flashcards
- Reader 1: *The Zoo*

Teaching Tips:

Make note of the **z** at the beginning of a word and **zz** used at the end of a word.

Introduction to Workbook Activities:

Review the alphabet story and the alphabet poem. Use the illustrations that go with the letters as flashcards. With daily practice the students will be able to recite the sentences and pronounce the words with the correct initial sounds. The students can color copies of the illustrations for additional reinforcement.

Review the alphabet. Introduce the letter **z**—the name, sound, and shape. Make note of the sharp points on the letter so it is not reversed or confused with the letter **s**. Have the students recognize the pictures and repeat so the beginning so the sound is distinct. Study the pictures used to identify the consonant sound of **z**.

Pictures: **zebra, zoo, zipper, zither, zero**

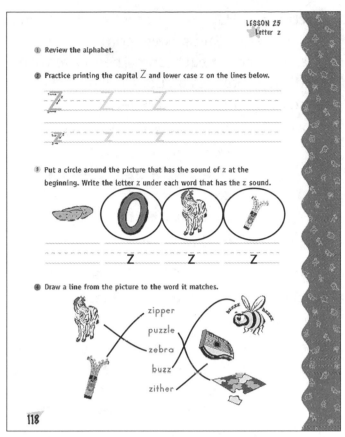

Activities 1 & 2. Review the alphabet. Discuss the beginning and the formation of the letter **z**. Be sure the student prints the letter **z** with sharp points and starts from left to right to avoid reversals. Print the capital **Z** and lowercase letter **z**.

Activity 3. Identify the pictures so the sound of **z** is distinct. The student will put a circle around the pictures that start with the sound of **z**. Print the letter **z** under the picture with that sound.

Pictures: **yam, zero, zebra, zipper**

Activity 4. Identify the pictures so the sound of **z** is distinct. Draw a line from the picture to the word it matches.

Pictures: **zebra, buzz, zipper, zither, puzzle**

Activity 5. Have the student read the sentences silently and answer comprehension questions about each one. Then have them read the sentences aloud. Underline the words beginning with the letter **z**.

> Sentences: **Dan went to the zoo.**
> **The zipper is bad.**
> **The zebra had a pen at the zoo.**
> **Tom has a zither.**

Activity 6. Read the make-up words.

> Make-up Words: **zim, zot, zig, zun, zeb**

Activity 7. Read the funny question sentences together.

> Sentences: **Can a zebra yawn?**
> **Is a zipper yellow?**
> **Can a zither run?**
> **Is the zoo big or little?**

Activity 8. Underline the words that **end** in the letter **z**. Note that at the end of some words there is a double **z** which does not affect the sound.

> Words: **buzz, fuzz, mat, fizz, mess, fez**

Activity 9. Read the words that **start** with the consonant **z**. Print the words on the lines below.

> Words: **zoo, zither, zipper**
> **zebra, zoom, zero**
> **zeppelin, zucchini**
> **zigzag**

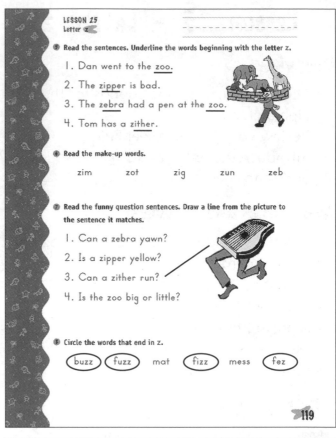

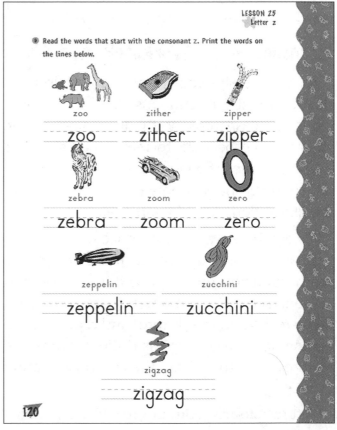

Activity 10. Read the words in the word bank together and discuss the meaning of each. Read the sentences together and try the various words for each blank. Student will print the words in the blanks to make a complete sentence.

Sentences: Jeb went to the (**zoo**).
The (**zebra**) is not hot.
Can you zip the (**zipper**)?
This is a (**zero**).

Activity 11. Practice printing the following phrases.

Phrases: **a little yard for the tot
a big yak
yellow yarn
a red yo-yo
a zebra at the zoo
zip or a zero
a big zipper**

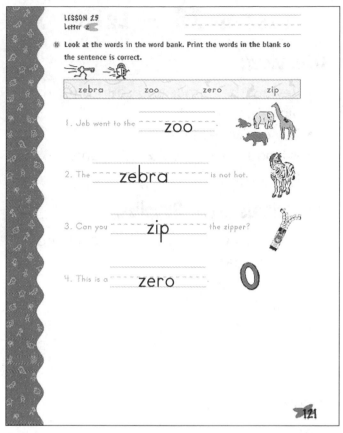

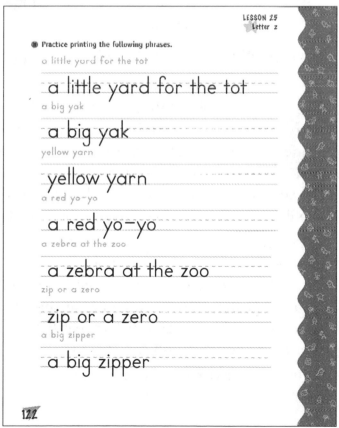

Lesson 26 - Letter x

Overview:

- Review the names and sounds for the alphabet studied
- Review Vowel Rule
- Introduce the letter **x**—its name, sound, and shape

Materials and Supplies:

- Teacher's Guide & Student Workbook
- White board
- Alphabet Story
- Alphabet Poem
- Alphabet flow chart
- Flashcards
- Reader 1: *"The X"*

Teaching Tips:

At the end of a word, **x** makes the sound of two blended consonants: **ks**.

Introduction to Workbook Activities:

Review the alphabet story and the alphabet poem. Use the illustrations that go with the letters as flashcards. With daily practice the students will be able to recite the sentences and pronounce the words with the correct initial sounds. The students can color copies of the illustrations for additional reinforcement.

Review the alphabet. Introduce the letter **x**—the name, sound, and shape. Have the students recognize the pictures and become aware that the sound of **x** comes at the end of the word. The student will repeat the words so ending sound is distinct.

Pictures: **box, fox, six, mix, ox**

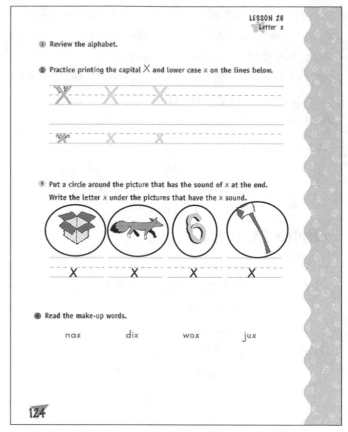

Activities 1 & 2. Review the alphabet. Discuss the beginning and the formation of the letter **x**. Have the students follow the number for directional clues. Note the difference in size and placement for a capital **X** and a lowercase **x**.

Activity 3. Identify the pictures. Put a circle around the picture that has the sound of **x** at the end of each word. Print an **x** under each picture.

Pictures: **box, fox, six, ax**

Activity 4. Read the make-up words.

Make-up Words: **nax, dix, wox, jux**

Activity 5. Read the sentences together. The student will underline the words ending in the letter **x** and then draw a line to the picture that tells about the sentence.

    Pictures: **Max will get six hens.**
                 The fox is in the den.
                 Can Mom fix the fan?
                 Dad can wax the van.

Activity 6. Read the funny sentences. Have the student note the question mark at the end of the sentence. Discuss if the sentence would be true or make-believe. Draw a line from the picture to the sentence it matches.

    Pictures: **Can an ox box?**
                 Can Jack sit on a fox?
                 Is Max in wax?
                 Can a fox mix?

Activity 7. Draw a line from the picture to the word it matches.

    Pictures: **Max, box, mix, fix, ax, fox, six**

Activity 8. Identify the pictures ending with the consonant **x**. Read the picture words and then print the words on the lines below.

    Words: **mix, box, six**

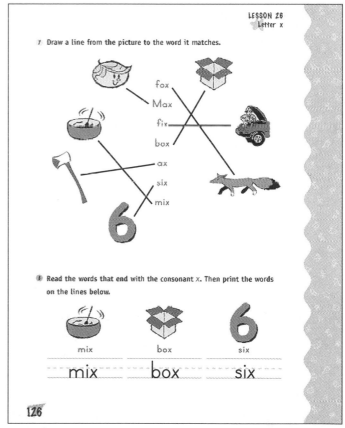

Activity 9. Read the words in the word bank together and discuss the meaning of each. Read the sentences together and try the various words for each blank. Student will complete the blanks to make a complete sentence.

Mom has a pan to (**mix**) the milk.
Max has (**six**) pet cats.
Can Dad (**fix**) the mop?
The (**fox**) sat on the hill.

Activity 10. Identify the pictures. Spell the words to match the pictures.

Pictures: **fox, fix, ox**

Activity 11. Practice printing the following phrases.

fix the sox
sit on a box
an ax can hit
a fox in a fix
Max Fox sat on a box
fix the x-ray

Lesson 27 - Consonant digraph th (beginning)

Overview:

- Review the names and sounds of the alphabet letters
- Introduce the Alphabet puzzle
- Use of alphabet flow chart if needed for sequencing
- Introduce the consonant digraph **th**
- Introduce rhyming words

Materials and Supplies:

- Teacher's Guide & Student Workbook
- Alphabet flow chart
- Alphabet puzzle
- White board
- Reader 1: *Thad's Math*

Teaching Tips:

The use of the alphabet puzzle is an activity for fun but will indicate if any of the letters should be re-taught. Explain the combination of the letters th is a sound that can be used at the beginning, middle, or end of a word. Make sure that the student is able to make the **th** sound successfully. In this lesson the emphasis will be on the beginning sound. Explain that rhyming words make the same sound at the end of a word. Use the white board to teach and demonstrate rhyming words.
Use the alphabet puzzle to verify if the student has mastered the letter names and sounds.

Introduction to Workbook Activities:

Introduce the sound of the digraph **th**. Study the pictures and have the student recognize the **th** sound at the beginning of each word.

Words: **think, thistle, thirty**

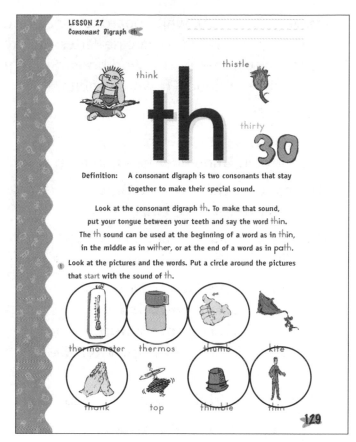

Activity 1. Identify the pictures. Make sure that the student is able to produce the correct sound of **th**. Student will put a circle around the pictures that have the sound of **th** at the beginning.

Pictures: **thermometer, thermos, thumb, kite**
thank, top, thimble, thin

Activity 2. Use the white board for practicing both the capital and lowercase letters before the student prints in the workbook. Student will practice printing **Th** with a capital **T**.

Activity 3. Practice printing the lowercase **th**.

Activity 4. Read the words together that start with **th**. Underline the **th** in each word.

> Words: **the, this, them, that,**
> **then, than, thin, thug**

Activity 5. Read the sentences together. Underline the **th** in each word.

> Sentences: **This fish is thin.**
> **The thumb is fat.**
> **That game is fun.**
> **Thad can hop. Then he**
> **can run.**

Activity 6. Read the make-up words.

> Make-up Words: **thub, tham,**
> **thos, theg**

Activity 7. Read each word and then print it on the lines below each picture.

> Words: **thumb, thimble, thirty**
> **thin, thank, thick**

Activity 8. Read the puzzle phrases together. Have the student draw a line from the phrase to the picture it matches. Point out that **path** has an ending **th** (this will be covered in more detail in Lesson 28.)

> Phrases: **a thick bug**
> **a thin thimble**
> **a thumb on a rat**
> **I thank God**

Activity 9. Use the white board to teach and demonstrate rhyming words. Student will read the words beginning with **th** and establish the ending sound of the written word. Study the picture and stress the ending sound of each picture. Draw a line from the rhyming word to the picture.

Pictures: **thin/pin**
            that/hat
            then/hen
            than/pan
            thank/bank

Activity 10. Read the sentence together. Discuss the capital **I** at the beginning of the sentence and a period at the end. Have the student print the sentence:

I give thanks every day.

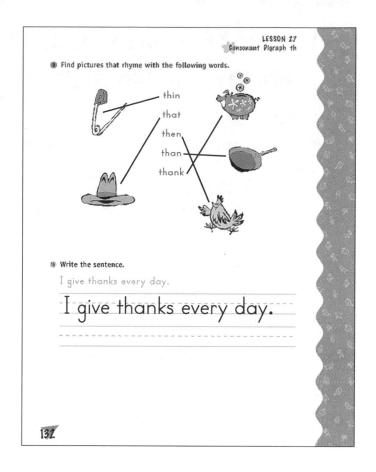

LESSON 27
Consonant Digraph th

⑨ Find pictures that rhyme with the following words.

thin
that
then
than
thank

⑩ Write the sentence.

I give thanks every day.

I give thanks every day.

132

Lesson 28 - Consonant digraph th (ending)

Overview:

- Review the **th** sound at the beginning of the word
- Review the **th** rule
- Introduce the use of **th** at the end of a word

Materials and Supplies:

- Teacher's Guide & Student Workbook
- Alphabet flow chart
- White board
- Reader 1: *A Bubble Bath*

Teaching Tips:

Present and review the rule for consonant digraphs. Review **th** at the beginning of the word. Introduce the use of **th** at the end of a word (**path** and **math**). Point out the need for a capital letter at the beginning of each sentence and a period at the end.

Introduction to Workbook Activities:

Review the rule for consonant digraphs. Print the digraph on the white board and have the student practice the sound. Reinforce that the sound is the same at the end as it is at the beginning of a word. Study the pictures and have the student recognize the placement of the **th** at the end of each word.

Activity 1. Study the pictures and have the student recognize the placement of the **th**. Student will put a circle around the **th** on the words below each picture.

Pictures: **tooth, bath, moth tenth, Beth, cloth**

Activity 2. Use the white board to print the words and discuss the placement of the digraph **th**. Have the students study the pictures and identify the **th** at the beginning or end of the word. Circle the **th** to show placement.

Pictures: **math, moth, Beth, thank teeth, thumb, path, bath**

Activity 3. Read the sentences together. Draw a line from the picture to the sentence it matches.

Pictures: **Beth can run on a path.**
I had a bath in a big tub.
The moth is red.
Thad is the tenth man.
The lad can do his math.

Activity 4. Reintroduce the use of a capital letter at the beginning of each sentence and a period at the end. Review the Capital Letter Rule. Read the sentences together. Have the student point out each capital letter and period. Print the sentences on the lines below.

This is the thumb on the hand.
The man had a gold tooth.

Activity 5. Use the white board to practice spelling. Emphasize the sound of **th** at the end of the word. Spell the words below the pictures by printing the beginning sounds.

Words: **(b)ath, (s)ixth, (m)oth, (p)ath**

Activity 6. Read the make-up words.

Make-up Words: **dath, buth, poth, foth, nith**

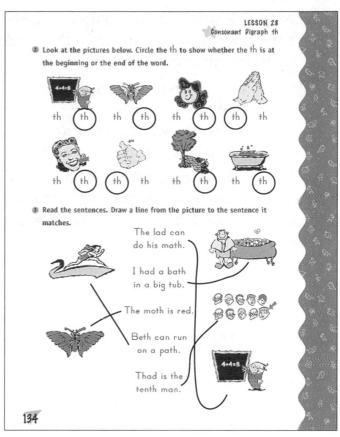

Activity 7. Read the puzzle phrases together. Have the student draw a line from the puzzle phrase to the picture it matches.

Pictures: **a path that led to a hat**
a moth on a dog
a fat cat with a thin dog
a pig with a math book

Activity 8. Emphasize the rhyming ending for each picture. Use the white board for reinforcement. Draw a line from the picture to the word that rhymes with it.

Pictures: **math/path**
dump/hump
pick/sick

Activity 9. Use the white board as an introduction to a crossword puzzle. Explain how the letter **a** will fit into both words. Use the sentences as a definition. Have the student fill in the missing vowel in the crossword puzzle.

Across: A place to walk. (**path**)
Down: Water to get you clean. (**bath**)

Activity 10. Read the sentence together. Have the student print the sentence on the lines below. Be sure to use a capital letter to start the sentence and a period at the end.

Sentence: **You can do the math.**

Activity 11. Read the sentence. Help the students with the ending **ck** in the word **rocks**.

Sentence: **The path has rocks on it.**

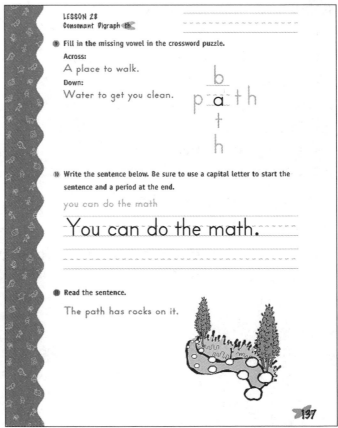

Activity 12. Use the white board to practice spelling. Emphasize the rhyming ending for each picture. Have the student spell the words below the pictures by writing the beginning sounds.

Words & pictures: **p**in, **f**in, **th**in
thank, **b**ank, **t**ank

Activity 13. Draw a line from the puzzle phrase to the picture it matches.

Phrases: **a thimble in a bath**
a path with a big bus

Lesson 29 - Consonant Digraph ch

Overview:

- Review the names and sounds of the alphabet letters
- Introduce the consonant digraph **ch**
- Introduce Proper Noun Rule

Materials and Supplies:

- Teacher's Guide & Student Workbook
- White board
- Alphabet puzzle
- Reader 1: *The Champ*

Teaching Tips:

Explain that the digraph **ch** is always spelled **ch** at the beginning of a word. It can also be used at the end of a word as in **church**. Introduce the capital letter as used for a person's name.

Introduction to Workbook Activities:

Review the rule for consonant digraphs. Print the digraph **ch** on the white board and have the student practice the sound. Note that **ch** can also be used at the end of the word as in much. In the word **church** the sound is both at the beginning and the end.

Activity 1. Study the pictures and have the student recognize the **ch** in the words. Student will put a circle around the pictures that start with the sound of **ch**.

Pictures: **chicken, check, chin, clock cherry, chips, chocolate, cheese**

Activity 2. Introduce the Capital Letter Rule for a person's name. Use the white board to print the student's name using a capital letter. Discuss the use of capital letters for family names. Have the student practice printing **Ch** using a capital **C**.

Activity 3. Use the white board to print other words that use a lowercase **c**. The student will practice printing **ch** using the lowercase **c**.

Activity 4. Read the words together that start with **ch**. Have the student put a circle around the **ch** if there is a capital **C** for a name. Put one line under **ch** if it is a lower-case **c**.

Circled: **Charlie, Chad, Chuck**
Underlined: **church, chick, champ, chin, chest**

Activity 5. Read the make-up words.

Make-up Words: **chid, dach, chep, chus, chob**

Activity 6. Read the sentences together. Review what a proper noun means. Have the student put a circle around each proper noun. Count the number of proper nouns you can find in all the sentences.

Chad went to the church with Ben.
I can put my hand on my chin.
Did Chuck see the chimp?
Can Charlie pick up the chick?

How many proper nouns were found? (**4**)

Activity 7. Read the words together. Have the student identify the pictures and draw a line from the word to the picture it matches.

Pictures: **chest, check, chick, chin, Chad, chimp**

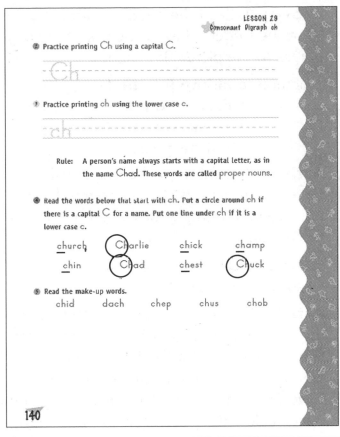

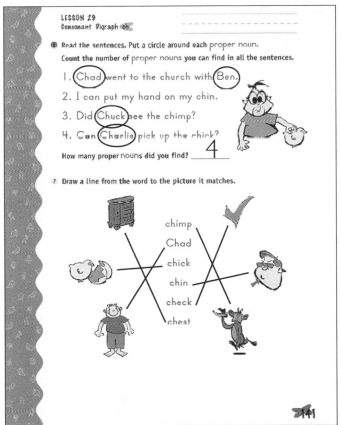

Activity 8. Read the puzzle phrases together. Have the student draw a line from the puzzle phrase to the picture it matches.

Pictures: **a chimp in a bed**
cheese in a tub
a chick in a chest
Chad on a cat

Activity 9. Read the sentences together. Have the student use the white board for practice in printing before printing in the workbook.

The chicken is in the pen.
I had much for God.

Activity 10. Study the pictures and discuss the meanings. Use the white board for practice printing. Emphasize the appropriate digraph at the beginning of each word. Have the student complete the spelling of the words below the pictures by printing the beginning sound.

Pictures: **ch**in, **ch**erry, **th**in, **ch**ip

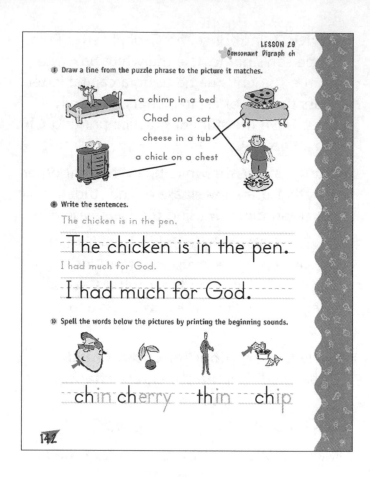

Lesson 30 - Consonant digraph wh

Overview:

- Review the names and sounds of the alphabet
- Review the Short Vowel Rule
- Review the consonant digraph sounds
- Introduce the consonant digraph **wh**
- Introduce question words and sentences

Materials and Supplies:

- Teacher's Guide & Student Workbook
- White board
- Alphabet puzzle
- Reader 1: *Ken's Toy Car*

Teaching Tips:

Review the alphabet letters and sounds. The alphabet puzzle and alphabet flow chart can be used as a check for the fluency of letter name and sound knowledge. To help remember the sound of **wh**, have the student put a finger to his lips and feel the breath that is blown when saying the sound.

Introduction to Workbook Activities:

Review the rule for consonant digraphs. Introduce the consonant digraph **wh**. Print the digraph **wh** on the white board and have the student practice the sound. This digraph will be used only at the beginning of the word.

Activity 1. Study the pictures and have the student recognize the **wh** sound in the words. Student will put a circle around the pictures that start with the sound of **wh**.

Pictures: **whip, hand, wheelchair, whiskers, whistle, whale, worm, wheat**

Activity 2. Use the white board for practicing both the capital and lowercase letters before the student prints in the workbook. Student will practice printing **Wh** with a capital **W**.

Activity 3. Practice printing **wh** with lowercase **w**.

Activity 4. Discuss the pictures and be sure the student recognizes the sound of **wh** in the word. Read the words together and student will draw a line from the picture to the word it matches.

> Pictures: **wheelbarrow, wheel, wheat, whistle**

Activity 5. Use the white board to practice spelling. Emphasize the beginning sound. Have the student spell the words below the pictures by printing the beginning sounds.

> Words: (**wh**)ale, (**wh**)iskers, (**wh**)eat

Activity 6. Study the pictures and discuss for vocabulary development. Have the student circle the pictures that start with the sound of **wh**.

> Pictures: **wheat, whale, thimble, wheelchair, whip, chin, whiskers, whistle**

Activity 7. Discuss the meaning of questions. Introduce the question words. As a joint project, make up question sentences using the different question words. Print the question words on the white board individually so they become sight words. Review the use of a question mark at the end of the sentence.

Activity 8. Review and repeat the question words with the student. Read together the question words and choose the best completion for the sentence. Trade asking questions and answers with the student for additional practice in question sentences.

Who/has the whip?
Where/did you fall down?

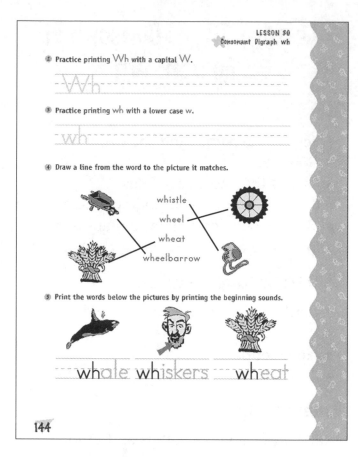

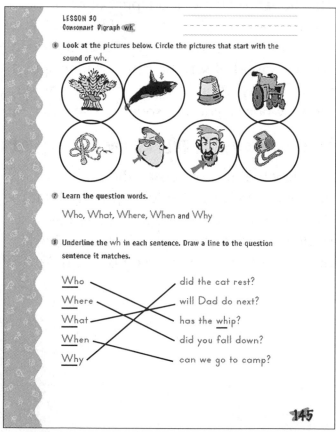

What/will Dad do next?
When/can we go to camp?
Why/did the cat rest?

Activity 9. Read the question sentence and the directions for the activity together. Have the student read the directions alone and then answer the question: "What is my name?" Give him the opportunity to print it on the white board first, then print it in the workbook.

Read the directions and question sentence together. Discuss the importance of knowing and being able to print one's own address. Check to see if the student knows the name of the street, city, state and zip code in which he lives. When that information is established, have the student print the answer to the question: "Where do I live?"

On the question above, **underline** the word **What**. Put a **circle** around the word **Where**.

Activity 10. Read the make-up words.

Make-up Words: **whan, whid, whem, whos, whuf**

Activity 11. Discuss and demonstrate using the beginning **wh** to make a word. Print several on the board as this activity is discussed. Allow a real word to be printed or a make-up word as above. Be sure the student knows the difference between the two and can pronounce it when he has it completed.

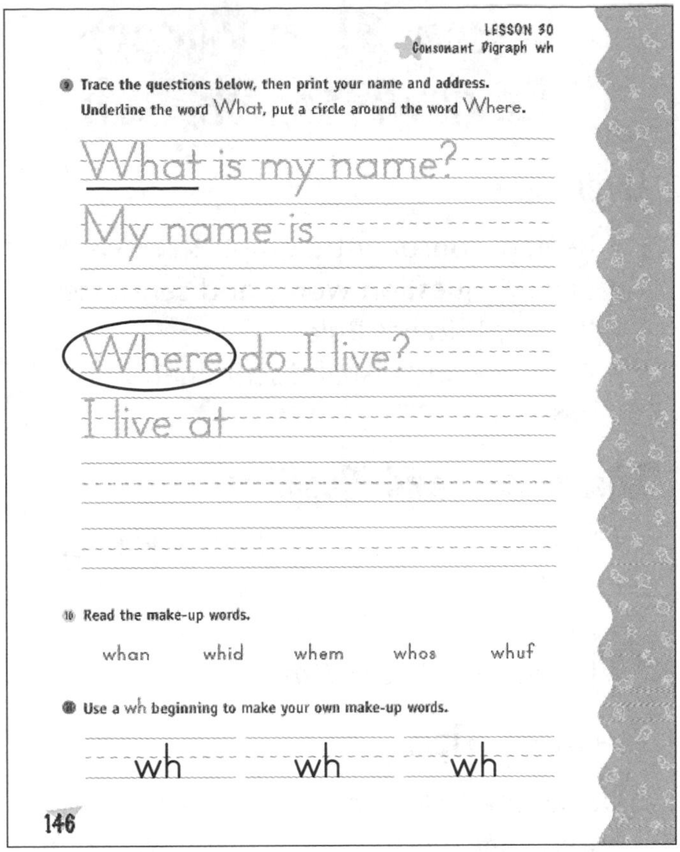

LESSON 50
Consonant Digraph wh

9 Trace the questions below, then print your name and address. Underline the word What, put a circle around the word Where.

What is my name?

My name is

Where do I live?

I live at

10 Read the make-up words.

whan whid whem whos whuf

11 Use a wh beginning to make your own make-up words.

wh wh wh

146

Lesson 31 - Digraph Review: th, ch, wh

Overview:

- Review consonant digraphs: **th**, **ch**, **wh**
- Review question words and sentences
- Review Phonics Rules
- Auditory and visual discrimination of words

Materials and Supplies:

- Teacher's Guide & Student Workbook
- White board
- Alphabet Puzzle
- Reader 1: *Chuck's Fish*

Teaching Tips:

Utilize the teaching tools of review to be assured that the student is ready to progress. The use of the white board, alphabet flow chart, and alphabet puzzle can be used in game form to confirm the student's knowledge of the alphabet names and sounds.

Activity 1. Put words beginning with **th**, **ch**, and **wh** on the white board and have the student identify the beginning sounds. Give verbal clues such as, "I'm thinking of a part of your face that starts with which digraph — **ch**, **wh**, or **th**?" Study the pictures that start with the sound of **wh**. Student will put a **circle** around the pictures that start with the sound of **wh**.

Pictures: **whistle, whiskers, wheat, sheep, chips, whale, wheelbarrow, thimble**

Activity 2. Review the beginning digraphs: **th**, **wh**, **ch**. Study the pictures and identify the beginning sound. This is an opportunity to develop vocabulary usage. Put an **X** on the pictures that start with the sound of **th**.

Pictures: **thank, wheelchair, thimble, thumb, thistle, thin, math, thermometer**

Activity 3. Review the beginning digraphs: **th, wh, ch**. Study the pictures and identify the beginning sound. Check vocabulary knowledge. Put a **square** around the pictures that start with the sound of **ch**.

>   Pictures: **chin, cherry, moth, chicken bath, church, check, chimney**

Activity 4. Read the make-up words.

>   Make-up Words: **chom, thaf, whid, chan, thub**

Activity 5. Identify the pictures and emphasize the beginning consonant digraph for each. Student will **circle** the consonant digraph that the pictures start with.

>   Pictures: **thimble, whale, chick, thistle, whip, cheese, thumb, wheel**

Activity 6. Study the pictures together. Have the student draw a line from the word to the picture it matches.

>   Pictures: **whistle, chair, thimble, thistle, child, thumb, whale**

Activity 7. Read one word from each of the boxes. Student is to circle the word you read, then print the circled words on the lines below.

Words:	**whip**	**when**	**whim**
	chap	**that**	**this**
	thin	**chin**	**when**
	chip	**with**	**chop**

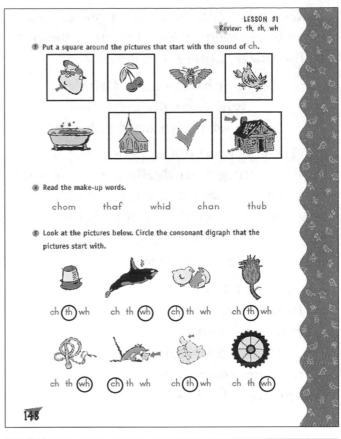

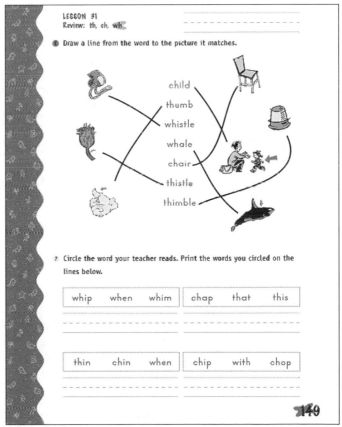

Activity 8. Read the puzzle phrases together. Have the student draw a line from the picture to the puzzle phrase it matches.

Pictures: **a thimble on a thistle
whiskers on a chicken
a whale in a wheelbarrow**

Activity 9. Read the sentences together. Have the student **underline** the words that start with the sound of **ch**, put a **circle** around the words that start with the sound of **th**, and put a **box** around the words that start with the sound of **wh**.

> **Jan is not thin.**
> **Thank you, God.**
> **Chad had a big chin.**
> **When can Sam get wheels?**
> **Tom can chop a log.**
> **Who has the whistle?**

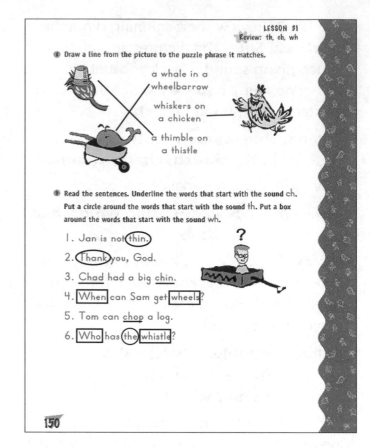

Horizons Kindergarten Phonics and Reading

Lesson 32 - Consonant digraph sh (beginning)

Overview:

- Review the names and sounds of the alphabet letters
- Review Short Vowel Rule
- Review the consonant digraph sounds.
- Introduce the consonant digraph **sh** at the beginning of a word
- Experience word search puzzle

Materials and Supplies:

- Teacher's Guide & Student Workbook
- White board
- Reader 1: *Shad's Toy Ship*

Teaching Tips:

Review the Short Vowel Rule and the consonant digraphs: **ch**, **wh**, **th**. Introduce word search activities as a game.

Activity 1. Review the consonant digraphs. Introduce the digraph **sh** as the "quiet" one. Demonstrate the gesture of quiet with the finger to the mouth in a whisper. This digraph can be used at both the beginning and end of a word. In this lesson the emphasis will be placed on the beginning sound. Study the pictures and discuss the beginning sounds of the pictures. Have the student put a circle around the pictures that start with the sound of **sh**.

Pictures: **ship, shelf, shirt, milk sheep, chin, shoe, shovel**

Activity 2. Use the white board for practicing both the capital and lowercase letters before the student prints in the workbook. Student will practice printing **Sh** with a capital **S**.

Activity 3. Practice printing **sh** with a lower-case **s**.

Activity 4. Study the pictures together. Some of the pictures may be used for vocabulary enrichment. Have the student put a **circle** around the pictures that start with the sound of **sh**.

> Pictures: **shirt, shadow, sheet, ship shell, shovel, thermometer, shed**

Activity 5. Review rhyming. Have the student read the words then draw a line from the word to the pictures that rhyme.

> Words/pictures: lip/**whip, ship**
> bath/**math, path**

Activity 6. Read the words together. Discuss the pictures. Student will draw a line from the word to the picture it matches.

> Pictures: **sheep, shoe, shave, ship, wheel, what**

Activity 7. Explain that this is a word search puzzle. Words that the students have been studying are hidden among other letters. Teach the students how to search according to directions.

> Across: **shell**   **shot**
> Down: **shed**   **ship**

Activity 8. Read the make-up words.

> Make-up Words: **shom, shen, shab, shig, shuf**

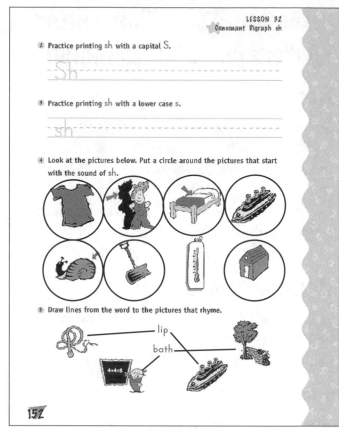

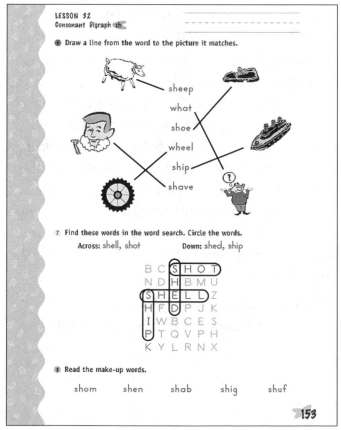

Activity 9. Read the sentences together. Have the student print them on the lines below. Be sure to use a capital letter for the first word in each sentence and a period at the end. Underline the words that start with the sound of **sh**.

    Sentences: **Sam has a big ship.**
                  Beth can get a shell.

Activity 10. Read the puzzle phrases together. Have the student draw a line from the puzzle phrase to the picture it matches.

    Pictures: **a shark in a tub**
              shave a pig
              a doll with a shovel
              a shoe on a shark

Activity 11. Study the pictures. Discuss beginning sounds. Have the students spell the words under the pictures.

    Pictures: **chip, lip, ship, rip**

Lesson 33 - Consonant digraph sh (ending)

Overview:

- Review the names and sounds of the alphabet letters
- Review Short Vowel Rule
- Review the consonant digraph sounds
- Introduce consonant digraph **sh** at the end of a word
- Review rhyming words
- Introduce alphabetizing words

Materials and Supplies:

- Teacher's Guide & Student Workbook
- White board
- Alphabet flow chart
- Alphabet puzzle
- Reader 1: *Shelly's Wish*

Teaching Tips:

Review Short Vowel Rule and consonant digraphs in the beginning of words. Introduce **sh** used at the end of the word. Review rhyming words and introduce alphabetical order. Use the alphabet flow chart and alphabet puzzle to reinforce alphabetizing of words.

Activity 1. Review the consonant digraphs. Introduce the use of **sh** at the end of words. Study the pictures and discuss the ending of the words with the sound of **sh**. Pay special attention the difference in the sound of **ch** and **sh**. Have the student put a circle around the pictures that have the sound of **sh** at the end.

> Pictures: **fish, bush, kiss, radish**
> **dish, dash, mash, cash**

Activity 2. Use the white board for practicing both the capital and lowercase letters before the student prints in the workbook. Student will practice printing **Sh** with a capital **S**.

Activity 3. Practice printing **sh** with a lower-case **s**.

Activity 4. Study the pictures with the student. Emphasize the placement of the **sh** sound. Discuss the meaning of the various words for vocabulary enrichment. Have the student put a circle around the correct **sh** to show whether the **sh** is at the beginning or at the end of the word.

> Pictures: **bush, shell, dish, fish ship, rush, shed, wish**

Activity 5. Read the make-up words.

> Make-up Words: **fash, dosh, mish, besh, dush**

Activity 6. Read the sentences together. Discuss the meaning of each. Have the student draw a line from the picture to the sentence it matches. Underline the words that end with **sh**.

> Pictures: **Dan fed mush to his cat.**
> **Can you push the dish back?**
> **Did Jan hush?**
> **I wish I had a check.**

Activity 7. Study the words in the word bank and discuss the meaning. Use the white board to review rhyming words. Have the student print the words from the word bank to match the words that rhyme.

hash/**lash, mash**
wish/**fish, dish**

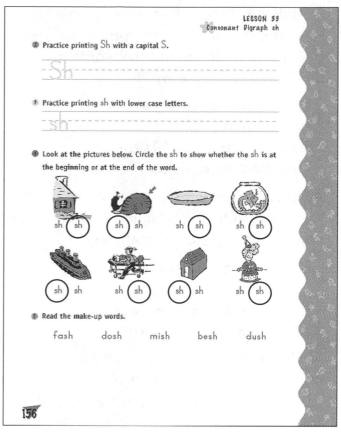

Activity 8. Read the sentences together. Have the student print the sentences and then put a circle around the words that have **sh** at the end of the word.

The dish is with a cup.
Is the shed red?
Ned fed mush to his dog.
Tom had to rush to see Ted.

Activity 9. Read the puzzle phrases together. Have the student draw a line from the puzzle phrase to the picture it matches.

Pictures: **a dish on a dog**
mash a ship
a bush in a net
a fish in a cup

Activity 10. Use the alphabet flow chart and puzzle to locate placement of words. On the white board, print the letters: **a**, **b**, **c**, **d**, spaced apart. Then read the words together and have the students print the word under the appropriate letter. As soon as the student is familiar with the idea, have him print the words in alphabetical order in the workbook.

Words (in order): **ant, baby, cat, dog**

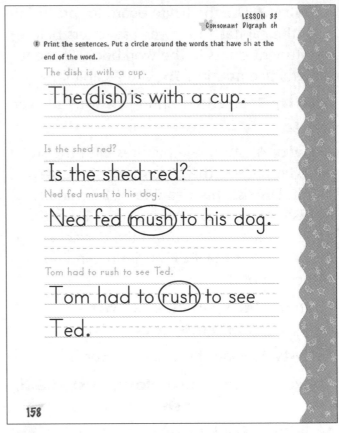

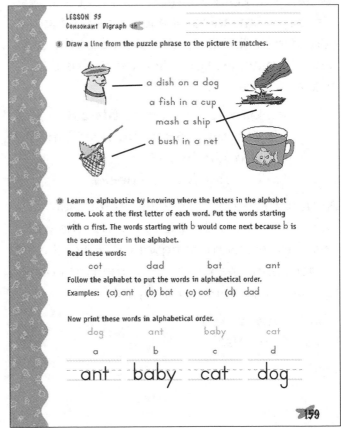

Horizons Kindergarten Phonics and Reading

Activity 11. Print each row of words in alphabetical order. The first letter of each word is given in its proper order.

Words (in order): **elf, fan, gate, hog
igloo, jug, kit, log
man, net, ox, pig
quit, rat, sit, ten
up, vest, web, x-ray**

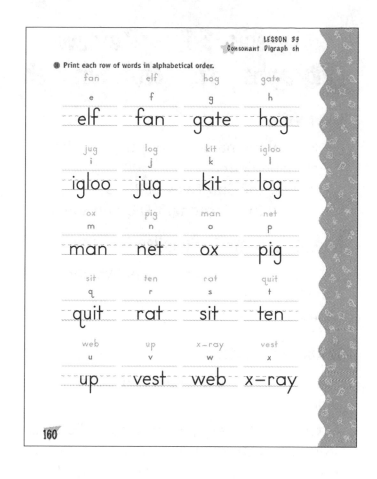

Lesson 34 - Review
Digraphs th, ch, wh, sh

Overview:

- Review the names and sounds of the alphabet letters
- Review the Short Vowel Rules
- Review the Consonant Digraph sounds

Materials and Supplies:

- Teacher's Guide & Student Workbook
- White board
- Reader 1: *Help for a Chick*

Teaching Tips:

Review Short Vowel Rule and Consonant Digraphs.

Activity 1. Review the consonant digraphs. Study the pictures and discuss the differences in the beginning sounds. Have the student put a circle around each picture that starts with the sound of **th**.

Pictures: **thimble, thistle, thumb, chin**

Activity 2. Have the student put a circle around each picture that starts with the sound of **ch**.

Pictures: **chop, check, cheese, bath**

Activity 3. Have the student put a circle around each picture that starts with the sound of **wh**.

Pictures: **chick, whip, whisper, wheel**

Activity 4. Have the student put a circle around each picture that starts with the sound of **sh**.

Pictures: **shed, ship, bath, shave**

Horizons Kindergarten Phonics and Reading

Activity 5. Read the words with the student emphasizing the final sound. Have the student put a circle around the ending sounds **sh** and **th**.

Words: **th – path, bath, moth**
sh – bush, wish, fish

Activity 6. Read the words together. The student will draw a line from the word to the picture it matches.

Pictures: **chick, bath, shark, dish, thumb**

Activity 7. Read the make-up words.

Make-up Words: **shup, chid, whaf, theg**

Activity 8. Read one word from each of the boxes. Student is to circle the word you read, then print the circled words on the lines below.

Words: **fish   fin   ship**
thin   math   chip
check   chip   when
whisper shed   whip

Activity 9. Read the puzzle phrases together. Have the student draw a line from the puzzle phrase to the picture it matches.

Pictures: **a fish in a bush**
a thin shark
a whale on the wharf
a check on a chick

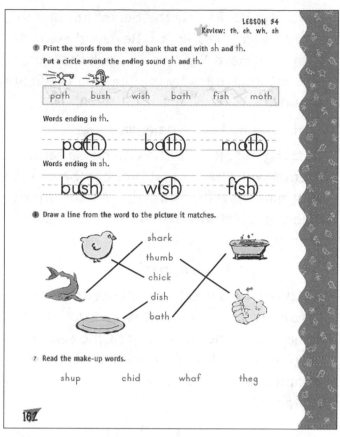

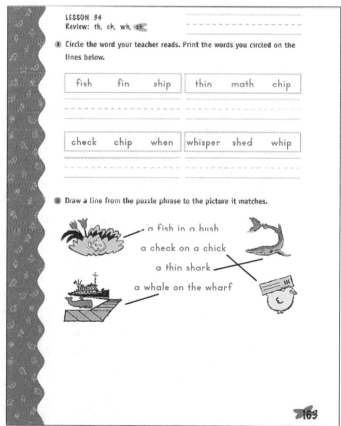

Activity 10. Review the beginning digraph sounds with the student. Review the words with him. Have the student spell the words below the pictures by printing the beginning sounds.

Words: **ch**icken, **wh**ale, **th**imble

Activity 11. Review the ending digraph sounds with the student. Review the words with him. Have the student spell the words below the pictures by printing the ending sounds.

Words: pa**th**, di**sh**, ba**th**

Activity 12. Read the sentence together. Discuss what the student would do if he had a ship. Have the student print the sentence on the lines below. Remind him of the use of a capital letter and a period at the end of the sentence.

Sentence: **I wish I had a ship**.

Lesson 35 - Silent e: ā ȩ

Overview:

- Review Short Vowel Rule to prepare for change to Long Vowels
- Introduce all long vowel sounds
- Introduce Long Vowel Rule
- Introduce diacritical marking for long vowel sounds
- Introduce familiar word families
- Compare short and long vowels

Materials and Supplies:

- Teacher's Guide & Student Workbook
- White board
- Reader 1: *Kate's Pockets*

Teaching Tips:

Teach the Silent **e** Rule. Introduce familiar word families with **a** and the silent **e**: **ame, ase, ave, ake, ape, ane, ade, ate, afe**. Explain the difference between short and long **a** sound in word change: **cap – cape**.

Introduction to Workbook Activities:

List all the long vowels on the white board with the diacritical marking. Teach the following Silent **e** Rule:

When two vowels are close together in a word, the FIRST one says its own name and the other one is silent as in **cake**, **bike**, **bone** and **tube**. Teach the students to watch for the clue of a silent **e** at the end of the word. Use the diacritical markings with a crossed-out **e** and a straight line (macron) above the first vowel.

Activity 1. Study the pictures together and discuss the meanings for vocabulary development. Discuss family endings: **ame, ase, ave, ake, ane**. Have the student put a circle around those that have the long **a** sound.

Pictures: **game, vase, cat, wave, cane, rake, cake, pan**

Activity 2. On the white board, demonstrate crossing out the silent **e** and putting a macron over the vowel **a** (**ā**) to show it has the long **a** sound. Have the student cross out the silent **e** and put a straight line over the long **a**. Encourage them to verbalize their actions as they do the activity.

Words: **rake, game, cake, wave**

Activity 3. On the white board, have the student print words with short **a**, then add the silent **e**. As soon as they understand the concept, have the student print the words in the workbook, using the diacritical marking to cross out the **e** and make a straight line over the long vowel **a**.

Short Vowel Words: **mat, rat, tap**
cap, Jan, pal

Activity 4. Read the words in Activity 3 with the silent **e**.

Activities 5 & 6. Have the student read the words and discuss the sound of short **a**. Student will read then print the words with the short **a** and mark them.

Words: **can, mad, man**

Within the same activity, have the student look at the words and pictures with silent **e** added to the end of each word. This makes the first vowel long or say its own name.

Words: **cane, made, mane**

Activity 7. Have the student practice printing the words with silent **e** on the white board first. Make a game of covering the **e** and having them pronounce it as a short vowel sound. If the concept is firm, have the student then spell the words under the pictures in their workbook.

Words: **rake, cake, wave**

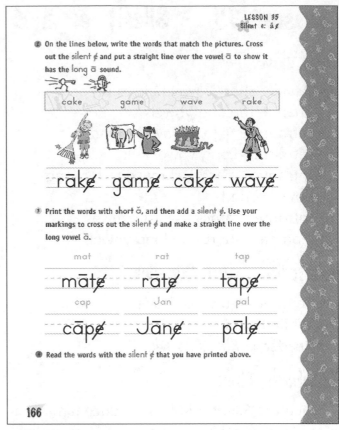

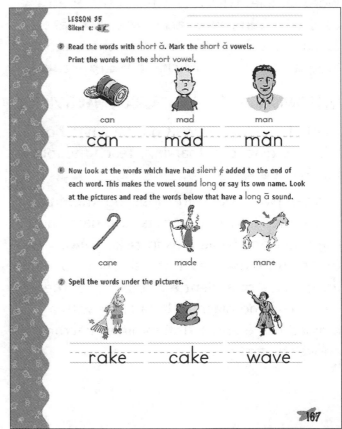

Activity 8. Read the sentences together and discuss the content of the sentence as well as the words with silent **e**. Make note of the silent **e** affecting the vowel **i** in the word **dime**. Have the student draw a line to match the picture.

Pictures: **Jane ate a big cake.**
Dave sat on a gate.
Dad will take me to the lake.
Jan put a dime in the safe.

Activity 9. Review family endings: **abe, ade, ale, ate, ake**. Continue recognizing diacritical markings. Discuss the pictures in each square. Each square has a choice of three possible endings. Have the student select and circle the correct ending.

Pictures: **babe, spade, cake**
date, whale, rake

Activity 10. Read the make-up words.

Make-up Words: **dabe, cade, fape, gake, tane**

Activity 11. Read the phrases and match up with the pictures.

Phrases: **a rake on a dish**
a cape on a can
a baby with a cane
tape on a rat

Activity 12. Read the sentences and words together. Have the student select the correct word to complete each sentence and print it in the blank.

I ate a (**cake**).
I can (**wave**) my hand.
The (**lake**) is big.

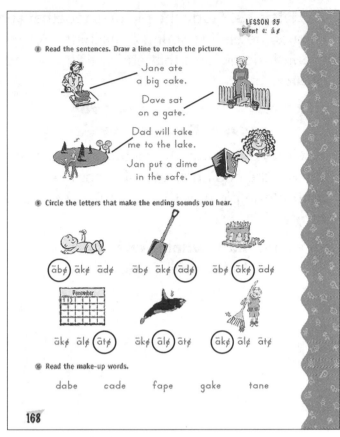

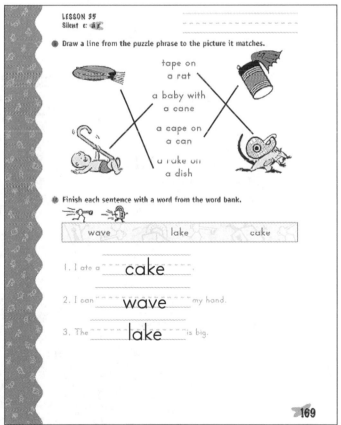

Activity 13. Study the pictures together and discuss the ending sound of each. Put a circle around the pictures that end with the sound of **ake**.

Pictures: **snake, lake, rake, rug cake, flake, make**

Activity 14. Study the pictures together and discuss the ending sound of each. Put a circle around the pictures that end with the sound of **ale**.

Pictures: **ball, whale, sale, tale bale, safe, male**

Lesson 36 - Consonant Blend bl

Overview:

- Review names and sounds of the alphabet letters
- Review the consonant digraphs
- Introduce consonant blend **bl**
- Review Phonics Rule
- Review Silent **e** Rule

Materials and Supplies:

- Teacher's Guide & Student Workbook
- White board
- Reader 1: *Where to Sit*

Teaching Tips:

When introducing consonant blends, emphasize that two sounds are blended into one sound. Use pictures of **black** and **blew** as examples using the blend **bl**. Have the student practice putting the two sounds blended into one. Use the white board to demonstrate using the blends followed by a short vowel and by a long vowel.

Activity 1. Introduce the consonant blend **bl** as two consonants blended into one sound. Use pictures of **black**, **blade** or **blend** to give practice to the blend **bl**. Discuss the pictures, their meaning and beginning sounds. Have the student put a circle around the pictures that start with the sound of **bl**.

Pictures: **block, blast, sheet, sheep blimp, blender, blade, Blake**

Activity 2. Use the white board to practice printing the blend with both capital and lowercase **B**. Have the student practice printing **Bl** with a capital **B**.

Activity 3. Practice printing **bl** with lowercase letters.

Activity 4. Study the pictures and discuss their meaning for vocabulary enrichment. Have the student print the words under the pictures if there is the sound of **bl** at the beginning.

  Pictures/Words: **blimp, path, blade dress, black, block**

Activity 5. Read the sentences together and discuss the meaning. Have the student draw a line from the picture to the sentence it matches.

  Pictures: **Can you blot the spot?**
     Sam has a black block.
     Did you see the blast?
     Blake can blink and wink.

Activity 6. On the white board, have the student practice putting the blend **bl** in front of various endings of words. When the concept is understood, have the student spell the words below the pictures.

  Pictures: **bl**ender, **bl**aze, **bl**ock
     Blake, **r**ake, **bl**ack

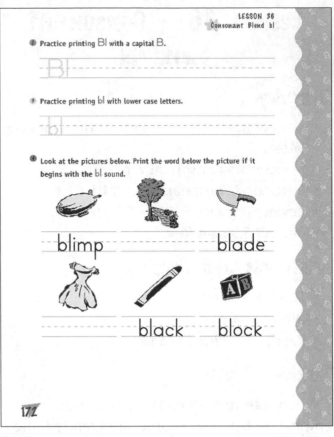

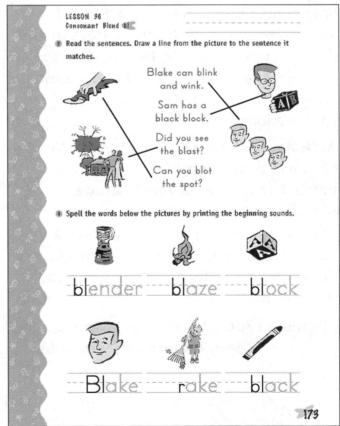

Activity 7. Read the words together, emphasizing the **bl** blend at the beginning of the word. Have the student draw a line from the word to the picture it matches.

Pictures: **bluff, block, blimp, blink**

Activity 8. Have the student read the make-up words.

Make-up Words: **blad, blef, blig, blom**

Activity 9. Read the puzzle phrases together. Have the student draw a line from the puzzle phrase to the picture it matches.

Pictures: **a blimp in a blender**
          a block on a pig
          a blade with an ant

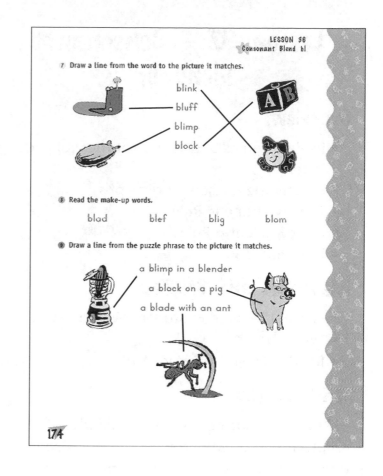

Lesson 37 - Consonant Blend br

Overview:

- Review names and sounds of the alphabet letters
- Review the consonant digraphs
- Review Phonetic Rule
- Review Silent **e** Rule
- Introduce **br**

Materials and Supplies:

- Teacher's Guide & Student Workbook
- White board
- Reader 1: *No Snakes for Me*

Teaching Tips:

When introducing consonant blends, emphasize that two letter sounds are blended into one sound. Use pictures of **broom** and **bride** as examples. Discuss the pictures, their meaning and beginning sounds. Use the white board to demonstrate using the blends followed by a short vowel and a long vowel.

Activity 1. Introduce the consonant blends as two consonants—**b** and **r**—blended into one sound. Use pictures **bridge** and **brush** as examples. Use the white board to demonstrate the blend **br** as the beginning sound when adding the remaining part of the word. Have the student put a circle around the pictures that starts with the sound of **br**.

Pictures: **brick, bridge, branch, shed brim, clamp, brush, brake**

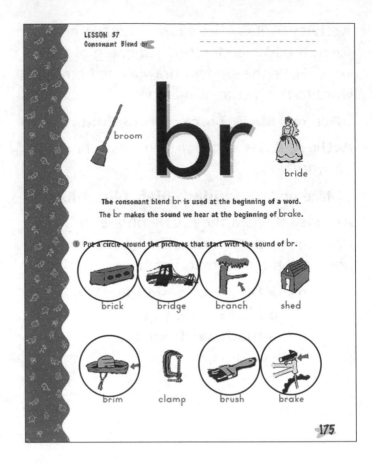

Activity 2. Use the white board to practice printing the blend with both capital **B** and lowercase **b**. Have the student practice printing **Br** with a capital **B**.

Activity 3. Practice printing **br** with lowercase letters.

Activity 4. Review the Silent **e** Rule. Read the words together to establish the ones that have the long **a** sound. Have the student cross out the silent **e** and put a straight line over the vowel.

Words: **brake, broke, blast, brave, brand**

Activity 5. Study the pictures below. Discuss the meaning for vocabulary development. Have the student determine if the picture begins with the sound of **br**. If so, print **br** below the picture.

Pictures: **bride, branch, ship**

Activity 6. Read the sentence together. Have the student print the sentence on the line below.

Sentence: **Brad had a little brush.**

Activity 7. Read the sentences together and discuss the meaning. Have the student draw a line to match the picture.

Pictures: **The brick is red.**
Blake has a brush.
Brad broke the vase.
Tom is brave.

Activity 8. Read the puzzle sentences together. Have the student draw a line from the puzzle sentence to the picture it matches.

Pictures: **Brad's pen is on his lips.**
Dan's cat sits on a brush.
Chad's leg is on a big branch.
Mom's cup is black.

Activity 9. Read the make-up words.

Make-up Words: **bram, bref, brib, brun**

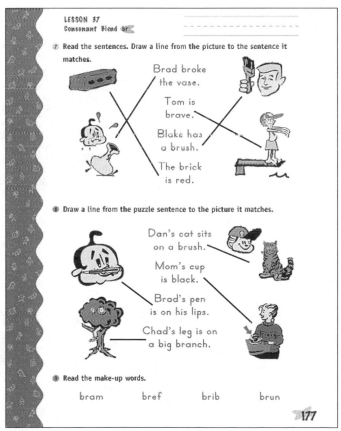

Activity 10. Use the white board to practice printing blends **br** and **bl**. Have the student spell the words on the board and then in the workbook.

Words/pictures: (**br**)ick, (**br**)ush, (**bl**)ock

Activity 11. Read the words and sentences together. Have the student choose words from the word bank that make the sentences complete. Use the pictures as clues.

1. Tom had the (**brick**) in his hands.
2. Sam can (**brush**) the dog.
3. The (**block**) was on the bed.
4. The (**bride**) ran to the path.

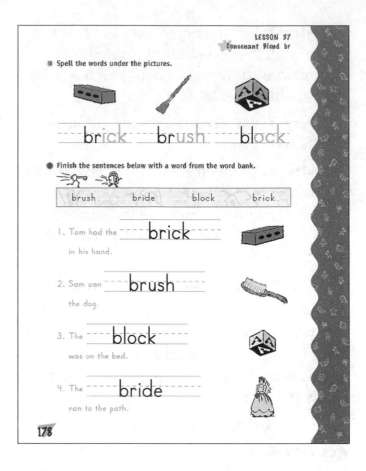

Lesson 38 - Consonant Blend cl

Overview:

- Review names and sounds of the alphabet letters
- Review consonant digraphs
- Review Phonetic Rule
- Review Silent **e** Rule
- Introduce Consonant Blend **cl**

Material and Supplies:

- Teacher's Guide & Student Workbook
- White board
- Reader 1: *Cool Off*

Teaching Tips:

When introducing consonant blends, emphasize that two letters sounds are blended into one sound. The picture of **clown** can be used as an example of the sound. Use the white board to demonstrate the use of the blend **cl** with the vowels following.

Activity 1. Review the Short Vowel Rule and the Silent **e** Rule. Use the white board to demonstrate the use of the short vowels following **cl**: **cla**, **cli**, **cle**, **clo**, **clu**. Have the students put a circle around the pictures that start with the sound of **cl**.

Pictures: **clock, candle, clown, ship**
clip, cloth, clamp, camp

Activity 2. Use the white board to practice printing the blend with both capital **C** and lowercase **c**. Have the student practice printing **Cl** with a capital **C**.

Activity 3. Practice printing **cl** with lower-case letters.

Activity 4. Study the pictures below. Discuss the beginning sound of each. Have the student complete the spelling of the word below the picture by printing the beginning sound.

   Pictures: **cl**ock, **c**ake, **cl**ap
             club, **cl**iff, **cl**own

Activity 5. Read the make-up words.

   Make-up Words: **clup, clis, clof, clen, clid**

Activity 6. Study the pictures and discuss the meaning. Review the beginning blends and consonant digraphs. Have the student put a circle around the letters that make the beginning sound you hear.

   Pictures: **cl**own, **bl**imp, **br**anch, **cl**ock
             brick, **bl**ast, **cl**am, **bl**ack
             thumb, **sh**oes, **ch**ain, **sh**ip
             thermometer, **ch**icken, **sh**ed, **th**imble

Activity 7. Study the pictures and discuss the meaning of each. Have the student review the choice of beginning sounds. Then print the beginning sound for each word below the pictures.

Pictures: **th**imble, **br**ick, **ch**urch
whistle, **cl**ock, **sh**oe
white, **bl**ade, **wh**eel

Activity 8. Study the pictures and discuss the meaning of each. Have the student draw a line from the picture to the word it matches.

Pictures: **clock, clamp, cloth, clip, clam**

Activity 9. Read the sentence together. Student will print the sentence on the lines below.

Sentence: **Sam can clap for Chad**.

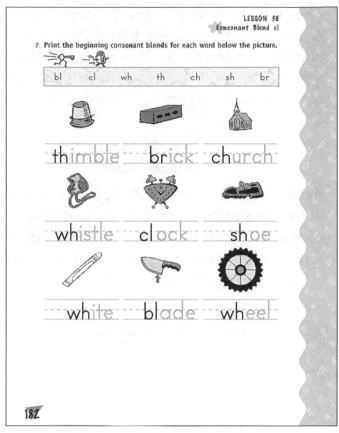

Activity 10. Have the student identify all the pictures and discuss their beginning sound. Practice printing on the board the beginnings and endings separately. Then have the student spell the words under the pictures in the workbook.

Pictures: **block, black, blast**
blink, blade, Blake

Activity 11. Use the white board for review of the consonant digraph sounds and the consonant blend **bl** sound. Discuss the pictures and the beginning sound of each from a choice of beginning sounds.

Pictures: **Bl**ake, **wh**ale, **th**ank, **bl**ade
block, **sh**ip, **ch**air, **bl**ink

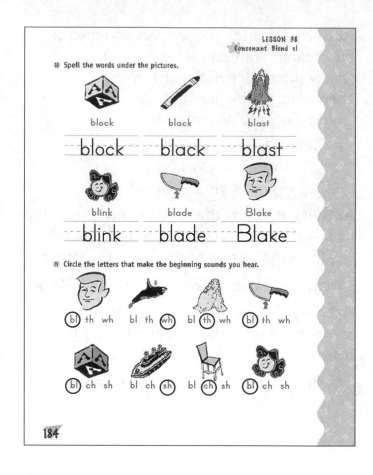

144

Lesson 39 - Consonant Blend cr

Overview:

- Review consonant digraphs and blends
- Review Phonetic Rule
- Review Silent **e** Rule
- Introduce Consonant Blend **cr**
- Review alphabetizing

Materials and Supplies:

- Teacher's Guide & Student Workbook
- White board
- Alphabet flow chart
- Alphabet puzzle
- Reader 1: *The Crab Story*

Teaching Tips:

Demonstrate the correct sound of **cr**. A picture of a crown can be used as an example of the sound. Use the white board to demonstrate the use of the blend **cr** with the vowels following.

Activity 1. Review the Short Vowel Rule and the Silent **e** Rule. Use the white board to demonstrate the use of the short vowels following **cr**: **cra, cre, cri, cro, cru**. Indicate that the Silent **e** Rule is used as in **crane** and **crate**. Have the student put a circle around the pictures that start with the sound of **cr**.

Pictures: **crust, clock, crib, crate**
chest, cross, crane, crack

Activity 2. Use the white board to practice printing the blend with both capital **C** and lowercase **c**. Have the student practice printing **Cr** with a capital **C**.

Activity 3. Practice printing **cr** with lower-case letters.

Activity 4. Study the pictures and discuss the meaning. Have the student circle the letters that make the beginning sound you hear.

   Pictures: **cl**ap, **cr**ust, **cr**ib, **cl**og

Activity 5. Use the alphabet flow chart and puzzle to locate placement of words. On the white board print the letters **a**, **b**, **c**, **d**, **e**, **f**, spaced apart. Then read the words together and have the student print the word under the appropriate letter. As soon as the student is familiar with the idea, have him print the words in alphabetical order in the workbook.

   Words: **elephant, fish, clock, dog**

Activity 6. Study the pictures and discuss the meaning. Have the students choose the correct beginning sound and print it in the space below the picture to complete spelling the word.

   Pictures: **sh**eep, **cr**oss, **wh**istle
             brand, **cl**amp, **bl**ack

Activity 7. Read the make-up words.

   Make-up Words: **crade, cren, crif, croz, crub**

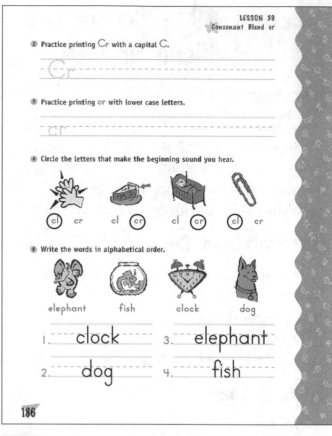

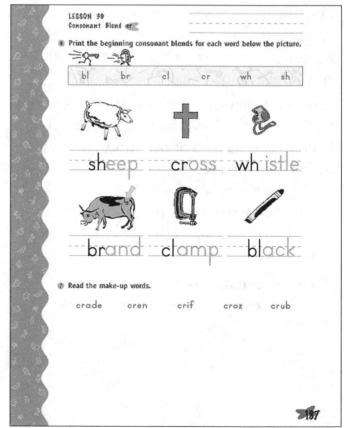

Activity 8. Read the sentences and words in the word bank together. Discuss the appropriate word to complete the sentence. Have the student print the words to complete the sentences in the workbook

>Sentences: 1. The (**clam**) had a shell.
>2. Blake can (**crawl**).
>3. The (**crane**) was in the lake.

Activity 9. Study and discuss the pictures. Have the student finish spelling the words under the pictures by filling in the beginning consonant blend.

>Words and Pictures: **cr**ack, **cl**ip, **cr**ib

Activity 10. Study the pictures and discuss the meaning for vocabulary development. Have the student print the beginning sound for each picture.

>Pictures: **cl**own, **cr**ust, **cr**ate
>**cr**eam, **cl**ock, **cr**ib

Activity 11. Read the puzzle phrases together. Have the student draw a line from the puzzle phrase to the picture it matches.

>Pictures: **a crack in the lake**
>**a crab with a cramp**
>**a dog with a crutch**
>**a crane with a crate**

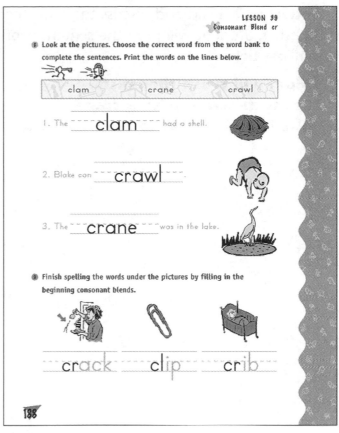

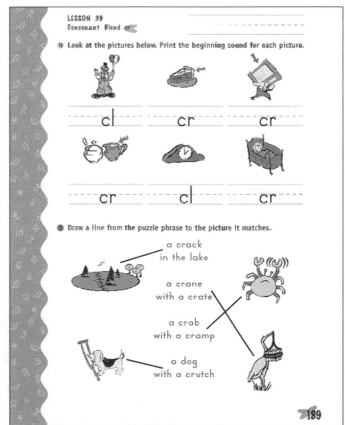

Activity 12. Read and discuss the sentences together. Student will print the sentences on the lines below.

Mom will crush the crust.
Cram the crate with a crane.
The lad will crawl to cross the crag.

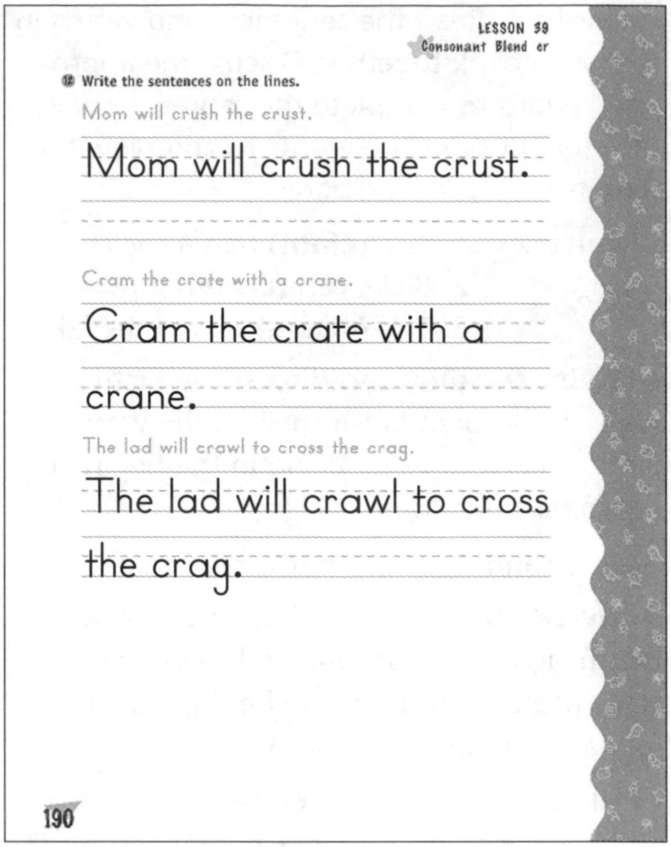

LESSON 39
Consonant Blend cr

⑫ Write the sentences on the lines.

Mom will crush the crust.

Mom will crush the crust.

Cram the crate with a crane.

Cram the crate with a
crane.

The lad will crawl to cross the crag.

The lad will crawl to cross
the crag.

190

Lesson 40 - Review
Blends: cr, cl, br, bl

Overview:

- Review names and sounds of the alphabet letters
- Review consonant digraphs
- Review Phonetic Rule
- Review Silent **e** Rule
- Review consonant blends: **bl, br, cl, cr**

Material and Supplies:

- Teacher's Guide & Student Workbook
- White board
- Reader 1: *A Crow's Brunch*

Teaching Tips:

Use the white board to review the consonant blends that have been studied. Expand the review with short vowels and words ending in silent **e**. Use part of the review time to have the student think of other words starting with those sounds.

Activity 1. Study the pictures and discuss their meaning. Have the student put a circle around each picture that starts with the given sound.

  Pictures: cr **clap, crust, crib, cross**
           cl **clock, clam, block, cloth**
           br **branch, crate, brick, bridge**
           bl **crane, black, blast, block**

Activity 2. Read the words in the word bank together. Have the student print the words in the row that is marked with the correct beginning sound.

  Words: br **brake, brad**
          bl **black, blue**
          cr **crate, crop**
          cl **clap, clock**

Activity 3. Study the pictures and discuss their meaning. Have the students draw a line from the picture to the word it matches.

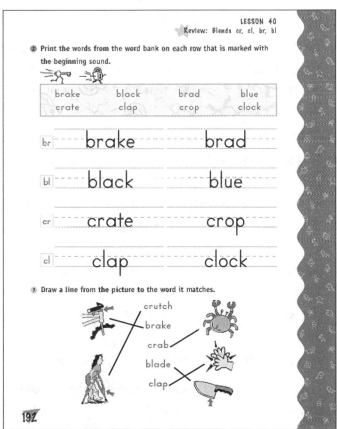

Pictures: **brake, crab, crutch, clap, blade**

Activity 4. Discuss the pictures. Have the student practice spelling the words on the white board and then spell the beginning sounds to complete the word in the workbook.

Words: **cl**amp, **cr**ate, **br**ide
black, **sh**ip, **th**in

Activity 5. Read the puzzle sentences together. Have the student draw a line from the puzzle setence to the picture it matches.

Pictures: **a clam on a clock**
a brush on a bridge
a branch on a cross
a blimp on a block

Activity 6. Read one word from each box. Have the student circle the correct word.

Words: **brake, brave, blade**
black, blade, blast
crate, crack, crib
clam, clock, clash

Activity 7. Study at the pictures and discuss their meaning. Have the student complete each word by spelling the **ending** consonant digraph.

Pictures: fi**sh**, bru**sh**, ma**th**

Activity 8. Discuss question sentences and question marks. Use the white board to have the student practice printing his name. Read the question sentence together. Again, mention the use of capital letters for a person's name. Have the student print the question sentence on the lines and then the answer the question by printing his name on the next set of lines.

Activity 9. Read the make-up words.

Make-up Words: **clob, crob, blom, brom,**
clof

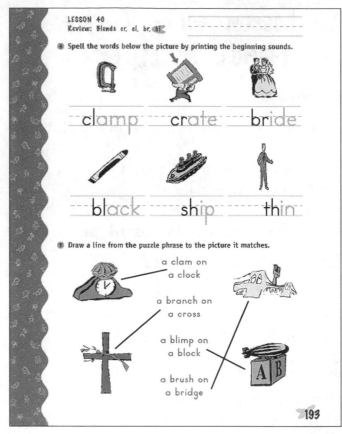

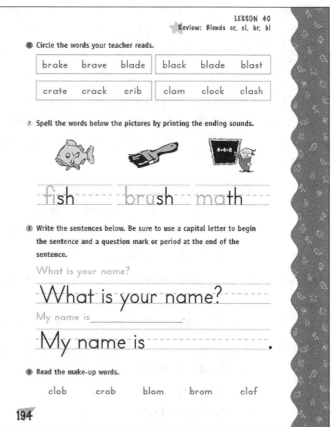

ALPHABET STORY

Andy Alligator was chomping down on an apple. His father, Alex said, "Andy Alligator, it is time to take a walk and have you learn the alphabet."

"I already know my name starts with the first letter — an 'A', and I know about the letter 'B' because Big Boy Bob has a baseball and a bat. Could we ask him to come with us?"

"Great idea," said Andy's father. "Let us go to the castle and see if we can find Candy Cat. She is usually eating catnip because she likes everything that starts with the letter 'C' like her name."

"Here is Dandy Doll all dressed up," said Andy. "What is she going to do?"

"That is a 'D' on her dress and she is going to dry the dishes."

They walked a little farther and saw Eddie Elephant looking in an eagle's nest.

"This is an 'E'" said Dad. "I think Eddie Elephant sat on the edge looking for eggs in the eagle's nest."

They came to Freddie Fish. He was trying to catch a football with a fork on the fence. He had the letter 'F' on his shirt.

Gary Goat goes golfing with a gorgeous girl named Gail. The letter 'G' was painted all over the golf ball.

"Hi," said Happy Hippopotamus, "can we play hopscotch? How do you like my new hat with the letter 'H' on it?"

"It is a honey!" said Andy's father.

"Look here. This is Iggie Inchworm itching by the igloo."

"He thinks everything that starts with the letter 'I' needs to be sent to an igloo. He has a family of insects and they are all going to get some ice and go to an igloo."

Jolly Jerry held a jumping Jack-in-the-box. It popped up, showing the letter 'J'. "Let me go with you and I will pop up any time you want," said Jolly Jerry.

Katie Kangaroo was flying a kite. On it was painted a big red letter K. "Kite flying is fun when you know that 'K' is for kite," said Katie.

Lucky Leo Lion said, "I am licking the letter 'L' off my licorice lollipop. You can have a lollipop when you know the letter 'L'.

Molly Monkey was making music for the merry-go-round. She said, "You do not have to have any money to go on my merry-go-round. Just know the letter M."

Nancy Nurse was counting nine nickels. "I know the letter 'N', said Nancy. "I would like to go along, too. I will save my nine nickels for later."

Ollie Octopus swung his arms around an ox and made a circle in the shape of an 'O'. "Here is an 'O' for octopus," he said.

Patty Pig painted a picture of a peach pie and said, "Since you know the letter 'P' for my name, I will give you some of my peach pie."

There was Quincy Quail feeding the queen under a quilt. Quincy Quail showed the food to Andy. "Each piece of food for the queen is shaped like the letter 'Q'. The queen likes that," he said.

Everyone saw Robbie Rabbit riding a rocket. "I am riding over a rainbow on this ranch."

"Come with us," said Sammy Sailor as he sat on a sailboat eating a sandwich and sipping a soda. "I have the letter 'S' on the side of my sailboat. I will share a soda and a sandwich with you."

Timmie Turtle heard them talking. "I am the teacher with a telescope watching ten tired turtles trotting. Look at this letter 'T' and I will teach you all the alphabet."

Uncle Umpire was under an umbrella and he was wearing his uniform. He had just finished umpiring a soccer game. On his uniform was the letter 'U'. "Let us join the gang and see if we can find that music I am hearing," said Uncle Umpire.

Victor Vulture was nearly all packed up to go on his vacation. Let me play this song on my violin. This letter is 'V' for a very fine violin.

They met Wandering Willie walking to the wigwam. "I have been following the path that looks like the letter 'W'. I need to find some worms so I can go fishing."

"This must be where 'X' marks the spot. Here is an x-ray and it shows some bones. The bones belong to Max Fox," said Andy Alligator.

"You are close to Yolanda Yellow," said Andy's father. "Here is her yellow yo-yo sitting on the letter 'Y'."

Zippy Zebra lives in the zoo. Here is a coat with a zipper and you can wear it if you know all the letters of the alphabet. Let us say them together:

ALPHABET POEM

A Andy Alligator eats an apple.

B Big Boy Bob has a baseball and a bat.

C Candy Cat lives in a castle.

D Dandy Doll dries the dishes.

E Eddie Elephant sat on the edge.

F Freddie Fish has a football on the fence.

G Gary Goat goes golfing with Gorgeous Gail.

H Happy Hippopotamus has a hat.

I Iggie Inchworm itches by the igloo.

J Jolly Jerry held a jumping Jack-in-the-box.

K Katie Kangaroo flies a kite.

L Lucky Leo Lion licked a lollipop.

M Molly Monkey made music for the merry-go-round.

N Nancy Nurse counted nine nickels.

O Ollie Octopus swung his arms around an ox.

P Polly Pig painted a picture.

Q Quincy Quail fed the queen under a quilt.

R Robbie Rabbit rode a rocket over the rainbow on his ranch.

S Sammie Sailor sipped a soda on his sailboat.

T Timmie Turtle teaches with a telescope.

U Uncle Umpire was under an umbrella wearing his uniform.

V Victor Vulture plays the violin.

W Wandering Willie walks to the wigwam.

X 'X' marks the spot on the X-ray.

Y Yolanda Yellow plays with her yellow yo-yo.

Z Zippy Zebra lives in the zoo.

Reproducible Illustrations for Alphabet Poem and Alphabet Story

Horizons Kindergarten Phonics and Reading

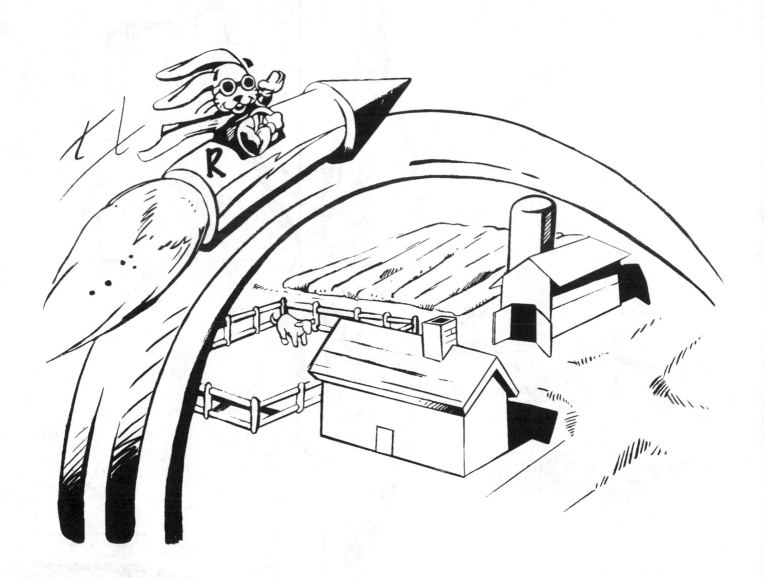

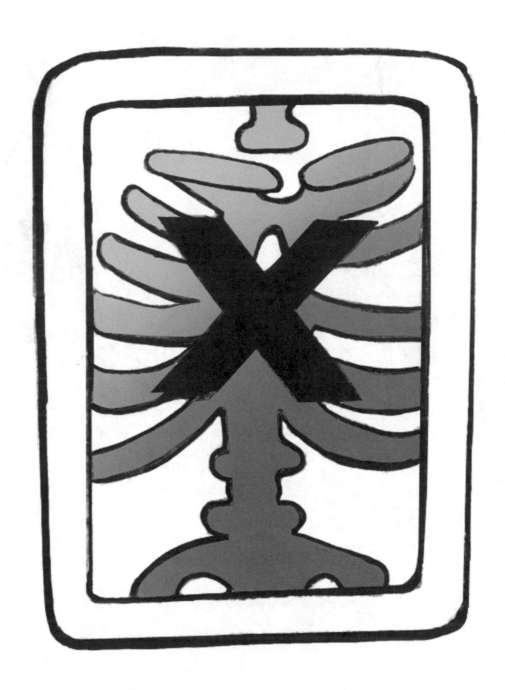

ZOO